# PLAGUE

BLACK DEATH AND PESTILENCE IN EUROPE

D1368880

# PLAGUE

## BLACK DEATH AND PESTILENCE IN EUROPE

WILLIAM NAPHY & ANDREW SPICER

TEMPUS

*Cover illustration:* A seventeenth-century depiction of St Carlo Borromeo ministering to plague victims in Milan in 1576. The frequency of flight by both Protestant and Catholic clergy meant that those who did stay, such as Borromeo in Milan or the Bishop of Marseilles in the eighteenth century, became saintly figures. (Wellcome Library)

First published in 2000 as *The Black Death*
This edition first published in 2004

Tempus Publishing Limited
The Mill, Brimscombe Port,
Stroud, Gloucestershire, GL5 2QG
www.tempus-publishing.com

British Library Cataloguing in Publication Data.
A catalogue record for this book is available from the British Library.

ISBN 0 7524 2963 9

Typesetting and origination by Tempus Publishing Limited
Printed in Great Britain by Midway Colour Print, Wiltshire.

# CONTENTS

# ACKNOWLEDGEMENTS

The authors would like to thank Jonathan Reeve and Tom Cairns from Tempus for their guidance and support during this project. We have been grateful for the assistance of a number of people in obtaining the photographs for this volume and for kindly granting permission for their publication.

In particular, we would like to thank Myrtle Anderson-Smith, Senior Curator, and her staff at the Special Collections and Archives, University of Aberdeen; Mike Craig, Reprographic and Bindery Services Manager at the Queen Mother Library, University of Aberdeen; Michele Minto and Helga Powell and the staff at the Wellcome Library, London; Fr F. Turner SJ, Librarian and the Superior of the Jesuit Community, Stonyhurst College.

Peter Ansell kindly sacrificed a rare sunny summer Sunday afternoon to photograph some of the illustrations.

WGN and AS,
*August 2000*

# One

# DEATH DIMLY RECALLED
## Epidemic Disease before the Black Death

*Thus saith the Lord God of David thy father: Because thou hast made Judah
and the inhabitants of Jerusalem to go a whoring ... Behold, with a great plague
will the Lord smite thy people, and thy children, and thy wives, and all thy goods.*

Chronicles 21: 12-14

n October 1347, a Genoese fleet arrived from the Black
Sea at the Sicilian port of Messina. The sailors on board
were already infected – dying or dead – by a seemingly new disease, a
horror, an affliction sent from God to strike down a 'third part of
mankind'. Scholars, physicians, churchmen, rulers, merchants, the
poor, the whole of Western European society cast about to explain
the dreadful destruction that had befallen them, their societies,
their cultures, their entire world. They looked to astrological signs,
to the conjunction of planets, the appearance of comets. Many spoke
of earthquakes and volcanic eruptions rending open the earth and
pouring forth evil vapours. The air itself seemed poisoned, everything and everyone corrupted and infected by the disease. Subsequent
commentators, chroniclers and historians have stressed that part of
the terror of the epidemic was its unexpectedness, its novelty, the
inability of medieval peoples to comprehend a 'new' thing.

*A woodcut from sixteenth-century France depicting the Biblical plague ravaging Egypt. Plagues, whether disease or natural disasters, were a sign of divine displeasure and were meant to punish sinful men and encourage a change in their behaviour.*

However, this is extremely unfair to the men and women facing the catastrophic pandemic that was the Black Death. In fact, they turned to their histories and the Scriptures in an attempt to find antecedents for the pestilence and to understand both how to contain and cure it. The reality was that there were a number of previous 'plagues' familiar to elite and commoner alike. Moreover, Christians had an interpretative framework within which to understand, if not combat, the affliction.

The most obvious place to which Europeans of the mid-fourteenth century would turn would be the Bible. Most notably, the children of Israel had been saved from bondage by the plagues sent against Pharaoh and the Egyptians for their duplicity and unwillingness to obey the commands of God through his prophet Moses. There was also the 'plague of leprosy' mentioned frequently in the

*This French illustration shows the Kingdom of Israel being devastated by a plague as a punishment for the sins of King David. The sins of a king, as the spiritual representative of the nation, could invite divine retribution.*

Bible. Both people and things (especially houses) could be infected and were ritually unclean (that is, unable to come before God and separated from His people). As the Israelites wandered in the desert en route to the Promised Land they were frequently threatened with or struck by plagues sent by God. The priestly caste was responsible for ensuring that God's Chosen People could come to Him atoned, protected from plague. When the people were unwilling to rely wholly on manna, or the spies sent into the Promised Land returned a pessimistic (and distrustful of God) report, or leaders plotted a coup against Moses and Aaron, plague was sent by God as a punishment for the wickedness of His people. When the people engaged in illicit sexual intercourse with infidels, 24,000 were struck down.

Anyone would be clear on the interpretation of these plagues. Disobedience and sinfulness invited plague. Divine wrath would fall upon God's people if the priests failed to atone for them and serve as proper intercessors. The Wrath of God, when turned against the people of God, for having 'defiled [God's] sanctuary with [their] vile images and detestable practices' would result in God ensuring that 'a third part of [the] people will die of the plague or perish by famine'. This prophetic threat was echoed in the apocalyptic literature of the New Testament where St John foretold that the Four Horsemen would ride forth to kill 'a third of mankind ... by the three plagues of fire, smoke and sulphur'.

Pious Christians could also consider the plague that God had sent against the Philistines who had taken the Ark of the Covenant and carried it off to the temple of Dagon, one of their gods. When they continued to insist upon keeping the Ark in the temple, despite the repeated overturning of Dagon's idol, God struck the Philistines with two plagues: 'tumours' and mice. The former was either haemorrhoids (in the Hebrew) or 'swellings of the groin' (in the Greek version). The latter was a plague of mice which attacked the grain supplies and the fields. Between the physical afflictions and the famine, many died. There is no reason to think that the Bible was referring to an outbreak of bubonic plague. Despite the Septuagint's reading, even the Vulgate is sufficiently clear enough to prevent anyone from equating the Philistines' 'swellings' with the buboes of the plague. In any case, the interesting part of the biblical story would not have been the symptomatic similarities but the causes of the plague. Nor should anyone conclude that the separate plague of mice would have led medieval observers to blame rats for their problems. The mice plague was clearly a distinct plague – the mice were swarming across the land (while any bubonic outbreak would have been preceded by a mass extinction among the rats). The Philistines were beset by plague and a mice-induced famine.

In other words, medieval Christians would not have looked to the Bible as a historical tool for diagnosis, the identification of symptoms, or any methodology for medical curatives and responses. The Biblical plagues would have been crucial for understanding the causal explanation for the epidemic. Why were people dying in their thousands? The Biblical stories were clear as an interpretative model. God was angry with His people, their religion and their priests. Plague was sent, not against individuals to punish specific sins, but against a people for general sinfulness and, especially, for incorrect religious behaviour. Idolatry, false worship, faithlessness – these invited sin. Only by repentance (the active alteration of behaviour and belief) could the plague be avoided or averted. Signs in the heavens, earthquakes, volcanoes might presage or even hasten plague but the cause was the Wrath of God incited by His people's sinfulness and faithlessness.

❖     ❖     ❖

The histories and medical treatises of the classical world were of greater use in a practical sense, though one must never forget that to the medieval mind, the identification of symptoms, cures and preventatives was no more important than the religious and spiritual identification of the actual cause (and therefore cure) of the epidemic. The classical world was not without information relating to epidemic diseases, pestilence and plague. Thucydides (*c*.460-*c*.400 BC) gave a detailed account of the plague which struck Athens during its war with Sparta. Although there has been much speculation about the identification of the disease, the reality is that there is no agreement as to the exact nature of the plague. What is significant is that the plague was identified as arising in Ethiopia then spreading through Egypt to Athens. The physicians were unable to do anything and died in large numbers while working with the afflicted. No specific treatment worked as 'what did good in one case did harm in another'. The disease was certainly contagious. Those who recovered were immune from a relapse. Society broke down to the extent that bodies were left unburned or were cremated en masse. Worse, Thucydides observed that men were gripped by a disregard for honour, the law or the gods: 'they resolved to spend quickly and enjoy themselves, regarding their lives and riches as alike things of a day'. 'Eat, drink and be merry, for tomorrow we die' became their motto. Although Thucydides reported that the plague came from Ethiopia and was therefore 'natural', he also said that some claimed it was the result of wells poisoned by the Athenians' enemies, the Spartans. For his part, Thucydides said, 'all speculation as to its origin and its causes, if causes can be found adequate to produce so great a disturbance, I leave to other writers, whether lay or professional [i.e. physicians].' The result was a bit clearer: the plague weakened the Athenians so greatly that it is considered one of the reasons for their eventual defeat by the Spartans.

This is not to imply that professional writers were not able to identify the symptoms associated with an outbreak of epidemic disease. Thucydides, while unwilling to state a cause or to hazard a name for the disease, did list the symptoms and Rufus of Ephesus (fl. AD 98-117) quoted Dioscorides (fl. first century) and Posidonius (*c.*135-51 BC) and said that the plague that had buboes was accompanied by a high fever, extreme pain, loss of physical self-control and delirium. Ancient writers, most notably Hippocrates (*c.*460-377/359 BC) via Galen (*c.*130-201), taught that epidemics (and most diseases) were caused by a poisoning of the air (miasma). These atmospheric poisons disturbed the balance of humours in the body and resulted in illness and even death. For the most part, these medical texts rejected any idea that pestilence was 'contagious'. The distinction is not always clearly delineated. The poisons in the air could 'infect' not only the air but also things (wool, cloth) which could 'absorb' the air. What was normally clear, though, was that people could not pass the disease from body to body. In that sense, plague was not 'contagious'.

Although classical literature might not answer the questions modern readers desire (for example, what exactly is the correct diagnosis of the disease under discussion), other sources as well as the Bible were able to provide medieval readers with a metaphorical understanding of the means by which epidemics were transmitted. Plague was showered down upon men by arrows fired from above. In the

*Iliad*, '[Apollo] let go a tearing arrow against the men themselves and struck them. The corpse fires burned everywhere and did not stop burning'. The imagery was the same in the Bible where God, in His wrath, said, 'I will heap calamities upon them and spend my arrows against them. I will send wasting famine against them, consuming pestilence and deadly plague'. To return to Thucydides, whatever explanation might be provided by 'other writers, lay or professional', the ultimate explanation of the cause of plague was obvious (God's Wrath) and the iconography (arrows) ready to hand for the artist.

Thus the distant past and the Bible provided the distraught people of 1347 with an interpretative framework for understanding the disease which was killing them in large numbers. The ultimate cause was the Wrath of God incited by the sinfulness of God's people. The metaphorical 'delivery system' was arrows rained down upon the afflicted. The medical explanation was a poison permeating the atmosphere. Presumably, therefore, the plague could be averted both by repenting of sin and cleansing the air – or fleeing an area of infectious miasma.

❖    ❖    ❖

What has been said thus far would lead one to infer that medieval people would have a framework for understanding any highly infectious, epidemic disease while failing to recognise the specific disease raging through their society. However, this would be to overlook one important feature of the history of Western Europe. The Black Death, and the recurring outbreaks of plague for the following four centuries, was in fact the Second Great Pandemic. That is, not only were there other epidemic diseases which had struck the greater part of Europe, but the plague had struck once before.

Before looking at the First Great Pandemic, it is worth remembering that most Europeans were perfectly at home with other epidemic diseases: for example, smallpox and measles. By 1347, these were primarily diseases of children (those who lived were immune). However, these diseases had struck with the ferocity of plague when they first reached the Mediterranean basin and Western Europe. Smallpox seems to have arrived in the period AD 165-180. Estimates are that the disease carried off a quarter to a third of the population of Italy. Less than a century later (AD 251-260), the Roman Empire was struck by the Antonine Plague (probably measles). Reports said that up to 5,000 people a day were dying in Rome at the plague's height. These diseases seem thereafter to have become endemic (native) to the population. Those without previous exposure (i.e. children) normally contracted these diseases while young and many died. Although the fatality rate may have been high among children, the overall death rate in the entire population would have remained very small. Moreover, these epidemics struck constantly. In other words, smallpox and measles were identifiable 'diseases' rather than plagues or pestilences. Since these diseases conferred a lifetime immunity, they were never able to kill on such a large scale. Their virulence, however, remained. When they were introduced into the native Amerindian populations of the Western Hemisphere the fatality rates were incredible, with estimates ranging from a 'low' of 50 per cent of the entire population to over 80 per cent.

The plague which struck the Mediterranean world in 541 was of a different character. It is this plague, the Plague of Justinian, which has been labelled the First Great Pandemic. For over two centuries (until *c*.760) the peoples of the Mediterranean basin were devastated by the cyclical recurrence of the disease. The consequences of the plague, both its initial outbreak and its returns, were dramatic. Indeed, if one considers the Black Death and subsequent plagues in the medieval and early modern periods as a watershed in European history (as many, if not all, historians do), then Justinian's Plague can be said to have had a similar impact on late antiquity. The Romano-Byzantine Empire under Justinian (*c*.482-565) was in the process of reconquering provinces of the Western Roman Empire (Gaul and Britain eluded his grasp).

Persia, the ancient enemy of the Eastern Roman (Byzantine) Empire was at bay. Then the plague struck. Estimates suggest that the capital, Constantinople (modern Istanbul), lost 40 per cent of its population (200,000 souls). In a subsequent outbreak (599-600), 15 per cent of the population of Italy and southern France died. The overall impact was a demographic collapse estimated at around 50 to 70 per cent over two generations.

The Eastern Empire was forced to withdraw its armies from the western Mediterranean to defend itself from barbarian incursions. Persia was likewise weakened. Trade was disrupted when the citizenry fled to the countryside or died. As the disease spread, villages and farms were abandoned. The economy was severely restricted by the decline in the population. Both the Byzantine and Persian Empires were highly centralised, trade-based urban polities. The disruption caused by the pestilence made it easier for the nomadic Arab tribes, recently converted to Islam, to sweep across much of the territory of both empires.

To understand the devastation and disruption caused, some comment must be made of an anecdotal nature. To this day, there are any number of Byzantine villages, villas, monastic communities and smaller provincial centres lying abandoned across Syria. These settlements were originally surrounded by cultivated fields but are now pastured and sparsely populated. Monks in numerous communities, who had managed to eke out an existence by careful husbandry and irrigation, had heavily populated the Negev Desert before the arrival of the First Pandemic, but afterwards their settlements were left empty and the land returned to desert as it remained until the end of the last century. Smallholders, who cultivated extensive fields of grain (which supplied the whole of Italy), had heavily settled in North Africa, especially Libya. The plague devastated the farms, allowing the irrigation systems to collapse and the deserts to advance. Not only were the trade routes throughout the Empire disrupted with the depopulation of the urban centres, but lands which had been extensively cultivated were left fallow and reverted to pasture at best and desert at worst. Most studies accept that the Middle East, Egypt and North Africa did not regain their pre-540 populations until the end of the nineteenth century. However, the recovery of the population was an almost wholly urban phenomenon and the rural countryside remains less populated (and less cultivated) today than fifteen centuries ago.

Nevertheless, although the Romano-Byzantines and Persians were seriously weakened and subsequently lost extensive lands to a nascent Islam, the civilisations were ultimately resilient enough to survive. Lands were lost to the plough, villages abandoned, urban centres contracted, but eventually trade recovered and the bureaucracies were able to remain substantially intact. That is, the structure of late antiquity survived. In time, alterations were made but even under the forces of Islam the most recent archaeology has shown that society and culture continued almost unchanged. There was no Dark Age between the First and Second Pandemics in the Eastern Mediterranean basin. In many cases the landscape changed and the imperial boundaries certainly contracted dramatically. However, the social structure and the cultural norms continued. This continuity is of great importance because it meant that on many levels the peoples of the eastern Mediterranean were historically prepared for the Second Pandemic. The disease, when it arrived, was a known quantity.

Christian and Islamic writers documented the path of the plague as it spread from Ethiopia via Egypt throughout the entire Mediterranean basin. Although there is some reason to suspect that this initial locus for the plague's generation is a literary and historical nod to Thucydides, it is probably actually accurate. Even the generally accepted calculation that 'a third of mankind' died probably is as much truth as literary convention. If anything, it might be an underestimation of the actual impact of the first plague. More important was the return of the disease every five to ten years in the East (Western European sources suggest a recurrence every nine to twelve years) until the mid-eighth century. For Western Christendom, the memorable outbreak proved to be that which struck Rome in 590. Everyone would have been aware of the miraculous salvation of the pontifical city by the Archangel Michael. Pope Gregory the Great (*c*.540–604) led a massive procession throughout the city and the plague ceased. The miraculous appearance of Michael sheathing his sword having slain the disease is still commemorated by the statue raised to honour the event on the top of Hadrian's Tomb. Castel Sant' Angelo, as the tomb was renamed, later became a fortress and is now a museum but the statue of Michael on the summit remains as a reminder of the miraculous deliverance of Rome 1,400 years ago.

❖     ❖     ❖

What explains the differences between the Eastern and Western responses to the plague of 1347? It is too simplistic to suggest that the distinction is purely the result of a religious difference between Islam and Christianity. Many parts of the East were still overwhelmingly Christian at the time of the second outbreak. Islam had taken over the medical and philosophical world of late (Christian) antiquity with little alteration. Indeed, the greatest distinction would seem to be levels of 'civilisation'. The East remained highly urbanised, cosmopolitan, and pluralistic while the West was a very backward, agrarian and extremely bigoted society. The rise of the crusading ideal had increasingly closed the mental world of the West, even as the returning Crusaders brought whole elements of Eastern civilisation back to their homelands. Moreover, the West seems not to have had a sense of social and cultural continuity with the world of Justinian's Plague, while the East had a civilisation and culture substantially unchanged from the world of late antiquity. The West was just on the cusp of the Renaissance and the 'rediscovery' of the ancient, classical world with its architecture, sculpture, literature, languages, histories, and cultural sensibilities. These needed no rediscovery in the East as, whether Islamic or Christian, this civilisation still existed albeit substantially altered.

Thus, writers and physicians in the East were able to turn not only to their holy books for understanding the Second Pandemic but also to their (shared) histories. For them, Thucydides, Galen, Hippocrates, Aristotle (384-322 BC), Plato (*c.*428-348 BC), Rufus of Ephesus, and the chroniclers of Justinian's age were all part of the same history. They were not lost or abridged, rather they were part of a continuous, yet changing, society and culture. Muslims were able to look back at the period after 540 and note that their historians told them of a string of five epidemics (of which the Black Death was but the sixth). The Plague of Shirawayh (627-628) had been followed by the Plague of 'Amwas (638-639), the Violent Plague (688-689), the Plague of Maidens (706) and the Plague of Notables (716-717). The lack of any outbreaks of the plague between the mid-eighth century and the mid-fourteenth was not considered of much (historical) importance. After all, the cultures of the East existed in a historical world stretching back millennia. What was a mere seven centuries in the great sweep of civilised history?

When the plague failed to return in the ninth and tenth centuries, the great Islamic civilisations of the Middle East, North Africa and Spain did not allow the memory of the events to recede ever more distantly into the past and, eventually, into oblivion. Rather, there was a massive explosion of Arabic translations and annotations of classical medical treatises. This was a concerted attempt to understand the disease, its causes and methods for preventing or curing it should it return. Western Christendom, when it finally 'rediscovered' classical civilisation and turned in the face of the Second Pandemic to its classical medical texts, has this period of Islamic investigation to thank for the survival of those texts and much of classical civilisation itself.

❖    ❖    ❖

Therefore, what can be said about the world standing unknowingly on the edge of the abyss which was the Black Death? History was able to provide various examples of plague. Everyone, whether Islamic or Christian, would have agreed that any great mortality was sent upon humans by the Divine Will. They would have shared the medical presuppositions of the ancient world with its emphasis on miasma over contagion. In other words, there was a vast area of shared views on epidemic disease, stretching from Gibraltar to the Persian Gulf and from Scandinavia to the Sahara. However, significant differences existed between the Eastern and Western worlds and the Islamic and Christian.

The most obvious differences are apparent when considering the conclusions drawn from the events of the First Pandemic by Christians and Muslims. Although both saw plague as an act of God, their understanding of God's motivation differed significantly. Muslims were advised by their religious leaders to react to plague in three very specific ways. First, no one was to flee from or go to a plague-infested area. Since plague was specifically and personally sent by God, no one could escape His Will and no one should attempt to place themselves in harm's way. Thus, plague was to be accepted and borne with resignation, humility and, because of the second basic tenet, with joy. Islamic thought also taught that, for believers, dying of plague granted immediate entry into Paradise. In that sense, there was no difference from dying of plague and dying on the field of battle during a Holy War or Crusade. However, although plague was a great joy and blessing sent by God upon believers, it was a punishment and judgement sent to infidels. Finally, Islamic thought completely and categorically rejected a theory of contagion for the transmission of plague. God had specifically and individually targeted the afflicted.

Christianity understood the appearance of plague in a much less specific and individual sense. Plague was a general punishment sent against everyone because of sin. In the East, Christians could understand this punishment as the consequence of the pluralistic, cosmopolitan world in which they lived. The East had numerous types of Christianity (which considered one another heterodox and heretical). Moreover, the success of Islam (often interpreted as an heretical form of Christianity by the Orthodox) was yet another 'plague' sent against Eastern Christianity and its Empire as a punishment and warning. In other words, plague for Eastern Christians could serve as a force of conservatism, leading them to conclude that what was needed was more orthodox belief. Rather than calling into question their presuppositions about themselves, the decline of the Empire, plague, defeat would all appear to be clarion calls to greater zeal, spirituality, mysticism and orthodoxy.

For Western Christians, the interpretative response was more complex. Christianity was fairly monolithic under the control of Roman Catholicism. Western Christendom perceived itself to be 'right' as opposed to the confused, heterodox and heretical world of the East. The East was decadent, or worse, under the sway of infidel Muslims. If the West was the last bastion of the 'true faith', then how was one to understand God's Wrath so obviously directed against the West by the plague? If Gregory the Great, one of the greatest exponents of papal supremacy and Roman Catholicism, had been able to end the plague, why had it returned? What was wrong with Western Christendom? Islamic thought could interpret the plague as a blessing upon believers and Eastern Christians could see it as a warning against any concessions in the on-going battle with heterodoxy, heresy and Islam. Western Christendom was perhaps forced to consider the introspective possibility that plague was a punishment for some internal and as yet unidentified fault. Thus, the same, shared historical and 'theological' world of epidemic diseases and medicine could – and would – lead the differing cultures of the Mediterranean and Western Europe to understand and respond to the Black Death in startlingly different ways.

# DEATH AT THE DOOR
## The Black Death and its Impact
### 1347–1400

*Oh, happy posterity, who will not experience such abysmal woe and will consider our history to be a fable.*

Petrarch

or the modern reader, stamped by the indelible imprint of the memory of the Black Death, it is difficult, if not impossible, to imagine the socio-cultural mindset of Western Europe in the century before the advent of the plague. However, if one is to understand the impact of pestilence, both 'actual' and 'psychological', it is essential to visualise and understand a world that knew nothing of the Black Death. Poised on the edge of a cataclysmic abyss, facing a catastrophic demographic collapse, a world of peasant farmers and urban merchants went about their daily lives accepting the recurring rhythms of the natural world and having no regard for Nature's world-shaking earthquakes. Society was oblivious of, and deaf to, the rising tide of laments that followed in the wake of the Black Death in its relentless march westward.

There is general agreement among historians that the Western Europe of *c.*1300–1340 was a relatively stable place but beset by a number of serious problems. With the slow recovery of the population after the First Pandemic, the peoples of the West were forced to bring more and more land, no matter how marginal, under the plough. Moreover, to supply that most basic of needs – bread – almost all land was converted to cereal production wherever possible. Thus, the population had reached the maximum number capable of surviving on the land available. Undoubtedly, this left many, if not most, people struggling on a subsistence existence – one harvest, or disaster from death. At the same time, research has shown that the climate was slowly worsening. The so-called 'Little Ice Age' saw increasingly severe winters and wet summers. The result was that many harvests failed or were unable to sustain people throughout the (longer) winters. This led to frequent famines with especially severe ones occurring in the 1310s. Although these conditions certainly killed many people, the population seems to have been able to recover fairly quickly.

The increasing pressures on the land from a large population created additional problems. A reliance on cereal crops tended to exhaust the land more quickly, as did the need to plant crops as often as possible (as opposed to leaving some land fallow). This tended to decrease the overall yield of grain. The mid-thirteenth century saw yields of 6-8 grains per seed sown with a ratio of 10:1 not unknown. With the sapping of the land's fertility, the ratio began to fall and has been shown to have reached levels nearer 2 or 3:1. In other words, instead of having five to seven, or even nine, bags of grain to eat for every bag of grain stored for replanting, many farmers were left with only one or two bags of grain to eat after reserving the seed for the next season's sowing. It takes little imagination to realise that this situation might continue to sustain the population, but left it extremely vulnerable to any fluctuations in the harvest.

For nearly two centuries, many historians have argued that this precarious balancing act in fact caused the great demographic collapse of the Black Death. This 'Malthusian' interpretation followed the views expressed by Thomas Malthus (1766-1834), an Anglican clergyman, in his *Essay on the Principle of Population* (1798). In brief, he argued that there was a natural limit to any population based on the ability of the land to provide food and other necessary resources. Once this level was reached, 'Nature' would intervene (violently) to decrease the number of people. This 'Malthusian check' might come in the form of war, famine or disease. This relatively simple, and seemingly logical, natural law meant that once the late antique world had reached its 'natural' limit, the First Pandemic struck to bring about a catastrophic decline in the population. At some point thereafter (from *c.*750), the population began to recover and had reached its natural limit by the mid-fourteenth century. Once again, the Malthusian check of epidemic disease struck, leading to a tremendous decline in population across Western Europe which was not completely reversed until the mid- to late nineteenth century. Thus, the effects of the First Pandemic took approximately six centuries to reverse while the Second left its imprint for a subsequent 400 years (assuming that the population began to recover around 1450-1500).

As appealing as this explanation might be, it is obvious that a number of problems are apparent. First of all, there is an attribution of direct action to the forces of nature. That is, Nature steps in to correct a population by the direct intervention of war, famine or plague. It is hardly surprising that an eighteenth-century clergyman might be inclined to posit a providential, nearly divine, power to nature. What is more surprising is the strength of this interpretation to the present day. One might well take the view that the Black Death (and the next century of plague, but not the following two centuries) was a Malthusian check. However, one would then have to assume that the two world wars and the Spanish 'flu of 1918-1920 were a similar check on an assumed over-population of Western Europe. As seemingly logical as the Malthusian law is in explaining the Black Death, its application to (modern) disasters brings down the whole house of cards.

More importantly than any philosophical and intellectual critique of Malthus, the details of the pre-Black Death world make it clear that even here the assumptions make no sense. The population of Western Europe had certainly reached a maximum level given the resources available. However, that level had been reached – and maintained – for nearly a century before the Black Death. Famines, over-working of the land, the worsening weather had all made life more difficult and had clearly increased the level of desperation in the lives of poor folk, but they had not produced a significant or sustained drop in the population.

The people of the West had attained a static level of population. This is not to imply that people were well or even reasonably fed. However, for all their poverty, they did manage to survive. To the extent that there was a check, it is much more realistic to view the situation as a ceiling rather than a guillotine. That is, the population had risen to its highest and through various active and passive means had stabilised. Malthus, by contrast, proposed that once the limit was reached Nature would intervene with a sweeping cull of the population. The facts make it clear that this had not happened.

This still begs the question of how a population had managed to reach so high a population level and then stabilised at it. Some check or checks were obviously at work, but what were they? Clearly the depletion of the soil's fertility served as a check in that it (and the weather) led to more frequent famines and a greater mortality rate. More people starved on a regular basis and, in some years, certain regions saw significant demographic decline; for example, some would suggest a decline of 10-20 per cent in the period 1309-1325. However, the effects were not permanent or pan-European. In addition, the actual amount of land available served as another check. There were only so many acres for ploughing and planting. The problem with a heavy reliance on either of these explanations is that they both tend to follow the Malthusian lead of attributing a certain 'intention' to the role of nature in population levels.

There were however, other checks on the populace arising from the people themselves. First, the constant subdivision of land into smaller and smaller plots with each passing generation led to an increase in a form of inheritance (primogeniture) which left holdings to a single child (the eldest son). This meant that younger children would not be able to support a family because they would have no land. The increase in celibacy, whether for religious or economic reasons, would have a direct impact on fertility and the overall increase in population. Indeed, it is perhaps worth noting that this period saw the Church placing greater emphasis upon celibacy for parish priests. While largely unsuccessful (in that priests simply took concubines), the problems of inheritance and the division of land to the descendants of priests was eliminated. They might have (illegitimate) children, but the lands of the Church would not be encumbered for their support.

Nor were individuals unable to realise that there was an actual limit to the number of mouths that could be fed from their possessions. There were a number of means available to the (non-celibate) individual to control fertility. The most obvious was to delay marriage until the couple was in a position to support themselves and their children. Thereafter, abstinence in marriage could be used to avoid children. Medieval people were certainly aware that delaying weaning a child tended to delay any subsequent pregnancy. There were also herbal remedies to inhibit (as well as promote) fertility. Finally, though, serious crimes, methods to induce abortion and even infanticide (and abandonment) were not unknown.

The simple Malthusian understanding of the Black Death must, therefore, give way to a more realistic understanding of the fourteenth-century world. Western Europe was extremely over-populated and this population was under intense pressure from the increasing dearth of resources and the worsening weather. Nevertheless, the population seems to have been relatively stable. A whole range of factors, both natural and human, had proved more than sufficient to maintain this stability. There is every reason to believe that this society and population might well have been able to maintain itself for an indefinite period. However, the reality was that while stable, the situation (and population) was also very precarious.

❖        ❖        ❖

In October 1347, this distressed, over-burdened society – balancing on the verge of subsistence and existence – was pushed over the edge by the arrival of plague at the port of Messina in Sicily. Its arrival inaugurated the cycle that characterised the movement of the disease across the continent. Usually, the disease would rage through the months of the summer and early autumn (depending on when it actually arrived). With the cooler months of winter, the disease would wane, only to re-appear the following spring. From the initial locus in a port, the plague would then spread into the rural hinter-land as well as to other ports where the cycle would repeat.

In the 1320s, the plague had broken out of the regions of Mongolia and the Gobi Desert where it was (and still is) endemic among the native rodents. It swept both West and East. Contemporary research has suggested that the outbreaks of plague in China (1331–53) killed perhaps 65 per cent of the population. In any case, by 1393 the overall population had fallen from 120 million to 90 million – a decline of 25 per cent in sixty years.

On its westward march, though, the plague first seems to have struck the Nestorian Christian communities of Issyk Kul near Lake Balkhash, where Soviet archaeologists documented a great mortality in 1338–39, including the discovery of three surviving tombstones giving plague as the cause of death. From here, the pestilence moved to Sarai on the Lower Volga in the Crimea in 1345. It was subsequently reported in Astrakhan (Azerbaijan) in 1346. Until it reached the Crimea, the plague had been moving overland, a journey that had taken nearly fifteen years. However, the plague now became waterborne.

There is a traditional story to explain how this happened. In 1345–46, the Genoese were under siege at the port of Kaffa (present-day Theodosia in the Crimea) by the forces of Yanibeg, the Khan of the Golden Horde. His armies were struck by plague and, in a desire to visit the affliction on his enemies in the city, he had the dead catapulted into Kaffa. The Genoese quickly cast the bodies into the sea. Despite their best efforts, they, too, were struck by pestilence. The assumption is that their ships, fleeing the siege, carried the disease into the Mediterranean world where it moved quickly along the sea lanes. If true, this early act of biological warfare rates with the impact of smallpox on the natives of central and south America and the gift of diseased blankets to the North American Indians by European settlers and conquerors. What is more likely is that the plague spread quite naturally from the siege camp into the city and, thereafter, among the Genoese sailors.

Whether by nature or the helping hand of Yanibeg, the plague struck the Mediterranean basin in 1347. In the Byzantine-Islamic East, the great sea ports of Constantinople and Alexandria were afflicted, as was Cyprus. However, the extensive network of trade routes, which criss-crossed the Mediterranean, meant that that same year saw the plague hit western ports as well. Messina in Sicily and the mercantilist naval powers of Genoa, Florence, Pisa and Venice were also infected. In 1348, other ports (for example, Marseilles) were hit. More importantly, the disease began to spread inland along the overland trading routes, striking the metropolises of Cairo, Antioch and Tunis, as well as inland areas of Italy (for example, Pistoia) and France (Montpellier, Narbonne, Carcassonne, Toulouse, Montauban, Bordeaux and Avignon). In 1349, Islam's great centre of Damascus lost nearly half its population. Indeed, although most readers may think of the Black Death as a (Western) European phenomenon, one must remember that the pestilence swept the whole of the Mediterranean world and carried off 30-40 per cent of the peoples of the Islamic Levant and North Africa.

The speed of the plague's progress was phenomenal and is a comment on the extensive trading routes across Europe. Not only had the epidemic struck inland areas in 1348 but it had swept across France along the major trade routes of the Rhône, Saône, Seine and Rhine rivers. The Low Countries were afflicted at Ghent, Bruges, Ypres, Brussels and Antwerp as well as northern France (Paris and Normandy). In addition, the pestilence leapt the Channel striking London, Bristol, Plymouth, Southampton, and its supposed first land-fall in England, Melcombe Regis (Dorset). The following year saw plague in Cornwall and Bergen (Norway). When Sweden was struck in 1350, the King, Magnus II (1317-74), said, 'God for the sins of men has struck the world with this great punishment of sudden death. By it, most of our countrymen are dead'. Western Europe's only crowned head to be taken by the plague succumbed in March of that year when Alphonso XI, the Implacable (1312-50) of Castile died while besieging Gibraltar.

By 1350, the disease had not only reached Europe's far north in Sweden and Norway but also its western extremities. Scotland, Iceland, Orkney, Greenland, the Faroes and Shetland were struck. Indeed, the plague seems to have been the final nail in the coffin of European settlement in Greenland, which had already been severely battered by climate change and famine; the Dano-Norse colonies were completely abandoned.

The epidemic had also marched across the Alps and down the Rhine, laying waste Switzerland and Germany in 1348-1350 and finally reaching Brandenburg in 1351. That same year the pestilence swept north and eastward into Russia, where the Grand Duke of Muscovy and the Patriarch of the Russian Orthodox Church both died from the disease. At long last the plague moved south into the Volga basin and the Ukraine. In effect, having raged west, north, east and finally south across the European peninsula of the Eurasian landmass, the pestilence almost returned to the Crimea whence it had broken forth in 1346, a scant five years before.

In its wake, Pope Clement VI (1291-1352) estimated that 23,840,000 people had died of a total population of 75 million – a

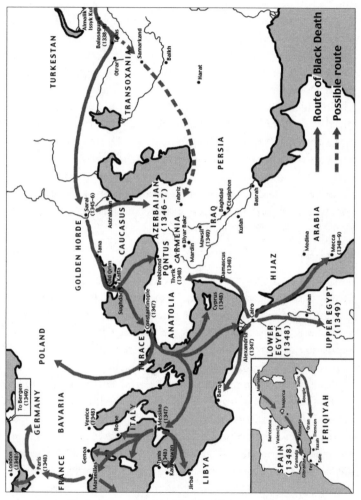

*A map showing the spread of the Black Death between 1338 and 1349.*

full 31 per cent. The only way to comprehend this level of devastation and death is to make comparisons with the modern world. To suffer a comparable loss, the present-day United States would have to watch nearly 84 million citizens die in five years. The European Union would need to lose a full 108 million and Britain almost 18 million (the population of Greater London and the South-East). The Chinese population would decline by 310 million, as would India. Overall, a world-wide demographic disaster on this scale would kill (in only sixty months) almost 1.9 billion people. In effect, one must imagine the entire population of India and China dying without a single survivor in five years. Death and disaster on this scale is simply beyond human comprehension or explanation – then or now. However, the preceding gallop through the chronology of plague gives some idea of the pace of the disease. To understand its impact, one must turn to the smaller scale of individual nations, cities and families.

❖       ❖       ❖

Some cities (for example, Venice) were hit very hard indeed. The best estimates are that between December 1347 and May 1439, between 72,000 and 90,000 people perished from a pre-plague population of 120,000-150,000, or 60 per cent. What is even more surprising than the sheer scale of the disaster is that Venice acted promptly to limit the impact of the disease. In many ways, Venice's location on a series of islands should have made it easier to prevent the entry of the disease into the city or, having failed in that, to contain it on infected islands. The city moved at the first sign of pestilence to impound all incoming vessels for a full forty days (hence the term quarantine from the French quarante, forty). The Venetian government also designated certain uninhabited islands as cemeteries, insisting that the dead be buried at least five feet deep. Despite prompt action, naturally defensible barriers and the strictest quarantine, the city not only failed to control or halt the disease but also suffered one of the highest mortality rates of any major city.

By contrast, Milan with a population of over 100,000 suffered only about 15,000 fatalities. Milan was a fairly sizeable (by northern Italian standards) state. However, it did not possess the excellent water barriers available to Venice. Presumably, Milan should have been easier for plague to enter and devastate. However, a number of differences might be conjectured. First, the government of Milan was under the firm hand of a powerful autocratic family that moved quickly to control the movement of people and goods into the city. Despite the best medical advice that the disease was miasmic, the Milanese state determined that it was contagious and acted accordingly. For example, any family showing signs of infection was walled inside their home. They had to be fed by baskets let down on ropes. Traditionally, this has been highlighted as a major factor in explaining the relatively few deaths in Milan. However, even a cursory examination would suggest that no matter what official explanation the Venetians had proffered for the plague, their actions would have been as successful against a contagion as anything done in Milan. One might proffer another possible suggestion. Milan, with its large rural hinterland, afforded places whither many of its citizens might flee, while Venice, locked on its overcrowded, damp islands was an ideal breeding ground for the plague. The reality is that no adequate explanation for the low rate of fatalities in Milan has yet been advanced.

The losses in London seem to have been fairly normative by European standards, if one can speak of normal in these circumstances. Estimates are that 25-50 per cent of the population died from a figure of 50,000 (that is 12,500-25,000 or between one in four and one in two). These 'headline' figures give little idea of the overwhelming scale of the mortality. In the two months from 2 February to 2 April 1348, a total of 2,000 bodies were buried in a single cemetery (or rather, thirty-four funerals per day, every day). Assuming ten hours of light per day in early spring, that represents a funeral every twenty minutes. Another example will suffice to highlight why so many felt their societies were being swamped by death. Between June and September in London, when the plague was even worse than in the early spring, 290 people were dying each and every day. These dead, many of whom would have required notaries and all of whom would have desired priests, had to be collected, their houses cleansed, the soiled, infected linens destroyed and funerals performed (assuming twelve hours of daylight, at the rate of twenty-four every hour – one every two and a half minutes).

While most cities seems to have lost about 40 per cent of their populations, one can gain some idea of the extremely high rate of fatalities by realising that many historians comment on the 'mild' plague that struck Antwerp and 'only' killed one out of every four or five persons (20-25 per cent). Although the actual numbers of dead in any city is on a more imaginable scale than the overall fatalities throughout the whole of Western Europe, one must not forget that mass death results in more than just bodies. Many industries and services in a given society rely on a certain critical mass of workers. Some activities simply would cease to be performed if 35 per cent of the workers died in a matter of months. Not only that, but manpower would also be required for a whole range of hitherto unknown functions. For example, there was an immediate demand for medical personnel. However, these were extremely skilled individuals who, if they worked in close contact with the afflicted, were likely to die faster and in greater numbers than members of the general populace. Societies beset by plague needed more than just skilled doctors. There was an immediate demand for plague workers, hospital workers, watchers (to identify those suspected of infection), and, especially, gravediggers. The dying would also have placed additional burdens on notaries (to make wills) and priests (to hear final confessions). Consequently, poor workers (including many women) drawn into contact with the dead and dying (for pay) and skilled, literate men whose professional services were demanded by the infected were likely to die in particularly high numbers.

One sees examples of the impact of the disease on the highly trained clergy from England. In January 1349, the Bishop of Bath and Wells reported that:

> The contagious pestilence of the present day, which is spreading far and wide, has left many parish churches without parson or priest ... Since no priest can be found ... many people are dying without the sacrament of penance [last rites] ... persuade all men ... that if they are on the point of death [to] make confession to each other ... [or] even to a woman.

Clearly, the good Bishop felt that so many clergymen had died (or fled) that even women were to be allowed to administer one of the most sacred sacraments of the Church. Although there was certainly theological support for allowing women to perform sacraments in emergency circumstances (especially the baptising of a dying infant at birth), the Church was not in the habit of advertising, let alone recommending, the practice.

Two specific cases, though, give us some idea of why the Bishop felt this move was necessary. When the plague moved into northern England (and Scotland), the diocese of York was ravaged. Over 40 per cent of the clergy are known to have died. If one assumes that some others might well have fled their posts, then one can surmise that many Christians, regardless of their medical condition, were without benefit of clergy in a time of dire need. The general disaster visited upon the Church is further illustrated by the case of the Archbishops of Canterbury during the plague. In May 1348, John Stratford died of the plague. A year later, without having been ordained to the archbishopric, Stratford's successor John Offord also succumbed. Within months, in August, the next archbishop, Thomas Bradwardine (1290-1349) died, too.

Again, while one must constantly bear in mind the personal tragedies these figures represent, it is also important to remember the long-term consequences of these losses. Throughout the peri-

od before the plague, the Church had been very successful in raising the overall standard of the priesthood and providing most
parishes with some clergy. Many parish priests had spent years at
university and were very well educated. Indeed, the rites of the
Church depended on a literate clergy trained in the use of a foreign language, Latin. Obviously, it would take any diocese many
years, if ever, to replace the loss of 40 per cent of its priests in a single year. Thus, a parish that fell vacant in 1348-49 because its priest
died could not expect a new clergyman any time soon. Moreover,
even were someone available they were more likely to be less well
trained, less experienced and, probably, much younger. Analysis of
the diocese of York bears out that the general levels of education,
age, and experience (in previous ministerial work) all declined dramatically after the plague and remained lower for many
subsequent decades.

❖     ❖     ❖

As dramatic as the scale of death was, there is every reason to think
that medieval Western society might well have been able to recover. However, as with the First Pandemic, the initial outbreak of the
epidemic (which is what the term 'Black Death' normally means)
was not a solitary event. By 1361, evidence suggests that the population was in the process of recovery. The return of plague in that
year resulted in a demographic decline of perhaps 20 per cent
overall. Thus, the second outbreak was perhaps half as virulent as
the first (the Black Death proper). This attack was followed in
1369-71 by a further outbreak of pestilence that is estimated to
have killed an additional 10 to 15 per cent of the population.
Thereafter, until the late fifteenth century, plague recurred every
six to twelve years.

The second outbreak (and subsequent plagues) differed in that it
was more confined to urban areas. One peculiar feature of the
Black Death was that it swept rural areas, as well as towns and

cities. Subsequent outbreaks tended to be localised in population centres. Nevertheless, the impact on rural areas was still great because towns and cities, in the immediate aftermath of an attack, tended to 're-populate' themselves with country folk. For example, around 1,300 villages were abandoned in England during the period 1350-1500, primarily through migration from the countryside to plague-blighted urban centres.

Thus the cumulative impact of plague, even when confined to the cities, was dramatic. The landscape itself changed. Villages were abandoned, farmsteads fell into ruin, fields were left fallow and slowly returned to nature. Wolves, which by 1300 had been banished to the far north, were found roaming the suburban edges of Paris by 1420. Fewer mouths required less grain, which allowed the remaining farms to diversify into forestry, cattle-rearing and wool production. Although grain prices seem to have held up rather well (the decline in production keeping pace with the fall in demand), prices for other agricultural products – such as timber, meat, wool, and leather – showed steep declines. At the same time, the collapse (literally) of the labour market meant that wages could rise. Moreover, tenant farmers were able to find attractive, well-paid work in towns and many abandoned their holdings. This increased the cost of rural labour and forced innovation in methods as well as the adoption of less labour-intensive forms of production (for example, shepherding instead of grain growing).

Specific trades were also forced to make alterations to traditional practices. The impact of mass mortality on the clergy has already been noted. Similar effects appeared in the various guilds. For example, periods of apprenticeship were shortened, younger men became masters, and trades recruited outside their familial groups. By 1430, the overall population of Western Europe, which had stood at 75-80 million in 1290, had collapsed to perhaps 20-40 million. At almost every level of society, this increased opportunity and mobility. Many trades were even forced, as was the Bishop of Bath and Wells, to look to women for assistance.

The cultural change this mass mortality created is most visible in the efforts of the traditional elements in society to halt, or at least slow, change. Numerous attempts were made to freeze wages and prices. Agricultural workers and tenants were ordered to stay on the land. Regulations (called sumptuary laws) were enacted, forbidding social classes from dressing and behaving 'above their station'. This implies that luxury goods such as silk were more widely available and affordable. Members of the elite were shocked to find that 'mere shopkeepers' were able to give lavish banquets, afford extravagant wedding feasts, be buried with immense pomp and, worse, dress their wives and daughters in great finery. The constant repetition of these laws simply highlights how useless they were in halting the dramatic changes taking place in society. The static (some might say stagnant), traditional, subsistence world that had existed before the plague had been blown apart. Although cracks had been showing before under the pressures of over-population, the decline in land fertility and climate change, the plague outbreaks of the last half of the fourteenth century accelerated the process at an unbelievable pace.

It is for these reasons that so many historians have considered the Black Death and subsequent outbreaks in the late fourteenth century as a turning point in Western European history. Earlier scholars credited the plague's impact with massive structural changes in society and culture. Cardinal Gasquet said it marked the end of the Middle Ages and the decline of monasticism in particular and Catholicism in general. Likewise, Coultan felt it led inexorably to greater wages and wealth and the subsequent Renaissance and Reformation. Thompson stressed that the psychological impact would have been greater than that left by the Great War (1914-18). However, notes of caution have also been raised against overestimating the impact of plague. Postan felt that the West was already in decline and crisis, and that the epidemics simply accelerated the process; a view echoed by Herlihy, Carperntier, Baratier and Bois. Shrewsbury even asserted that, contrary to the traditionally accepted figures, plague could not have killed more than 20 per cent of the English population. Finally, some historians (Jutikkala, Kaupinnen, Chambers, Hatcher, Biraben, Le Roy Ladurie) have stressed that the mortality of the plague was part of a greater schema of ecological crises spread over three centuries.

❖     ❖     ❖

In every sense, these historians are collectively and individually correct. Together, they simply reinforce the image of the Black Death as one of the major events in Western European history. Indeed, the Second Pandemic is one of the major events in world history, striking as it did China, the Islamic world and the Byzantine Empire. As Ibn Khald-un (1332-1406) recorded in his *Muqaddimah*:

> Civilisation both in the East and the West was visited by a destructive plague which devastated nations and caused populations to vanish. It swallowed up many of the good things of civilisation and wiped them out ... Civilisation decreased with the decrease of mankind ... The entire inhabited world changed.

Although one might be tempted to focus on the interpretations of modern academics, Khald-un reminds us that the people left alive by the pestilence were forced to provide their own explanations for the catastrophe and interpretations for its effects. How did medieval people respond to so many deaths? As the first chapter stressed, everything in their mental world would suggest that they would look for a religious or spiritual interpretation for the cause of the disaster, as well as a religious or spiritual response to prevent the return of the pestilence.

It is possible to delineate a number of responses. For obvious reasons, flight was perhaps the most natural reaction during an epidemic. The attack on Florence left a vivid example of this, as well as one of the world's greatest literary masterpieces. Fleeing from the disease, a group of Florentine men and women spent their time in voluntary exile telling one another stories, or so the events are reported by Boccaccio (1313-75) in his *Decameron*. Many of the stories he recounted highlight a second response that was perhaps longer lasting and certainly more psychological. Contemporary chroniclers noted an 'Epicurean' response to the Black Death: people simply took to the taverns and lived life as though each day was their last. Many reported that laws had become meaningless; men and women lived without honour or regard for their reputations and great emphasis was placed on luxury and riotous living.

The most obvious aspect of this response to flee or to indulge in excess is the contrast with any sort of religious reaction. One need only recall that Islam forbade flight, stating that God sent plague as a blessing and no one could, or should, flee God's Will. Although Christian theology never developed so deterministic an understanding of natural disasters, there was certainly some understanding that Christians (especially those in authority or in the Church) had a duty to remain at their post and care for the sick and dying. Flight, if not a violation of divine will, was certainly a betrayal of communal and civic responsibility. Epicureanism, on the other hand, was decidedly un-Christian. The emphasis upon present, temporal existence without regard to its eternal consequences was a denial of the faith. Not only was it lawless and dishonourable, it was also blasphemous and irreligious.

What could have led people to abandon their neighbours, their responsibilities, the law and their faith? In part, the collapse of civil structures simply made it easier for lawlessness and riotous behaviour to abound. That is, these 'Epicureans' may always have lived for the day, but their proclivities had previously been constrained by society and its conventions and laws. However, the near collapse of the Church might well have played a part. While many priests undoubtedly stayed and ministered to the afflicted until they, too, succumbed, many others fled their parishioners. Regrettably, humans being what they are, the image of one fleeing priest was more memorable (and worthy of gossip) than the ten who stayed and died in their posts. Many may have turned to the pleasures and pursuits of this life, having felt abandoned by the institutions and hierarchy of their religion. It is just as likely that the constant procession of the dead and dying moving through their streets had infected the living with a frenzy of fear and dread. Numbed by grief and despair, they may have been driven to excesses in an effort 'to feel alive, to feel anything'.

There were, however, many people who found solace in their religion. Indeed, the Black Death and the later outbreaks of the fourteenth century have often been seen as a spur to religious activity. One of the most obvious responses was to find ways of avoiding infection or, failing that, to prevent death. For this, people naturally turned to their religion for those to intercede on their behalf with God. As almost everyone would have been convinced that God was afflicting His people for some reason, appeals to God to avert His wrath were perfectly normal. However, people were unlikely to approach God directly. Their beliefs would have led them to rely on those with greater spiritual strength and grace to intercede or pray for them. In practice, the first person to whom they would turn was the priest. The plagues in the Bible had often been averted by the intercession of priests and holy men after the people had repented. However, with many priests dying, dead or missing, other religious figures with even greater power would have been sought.

Not surprisingly, the people did as they always did and turned to the saints. Medieval religion taught them that the saints had a special relationship with God because of their great holiness. Sadly, since over six centuries had passed since the outbreaks following the First Pandemic, there was not an obvious choice for a patron saint of plague sufferers. In part, the iconography of plague helped. The disease was visualised as arrows fired by God. St Sebastian (d. *c.*288) was the patron saint most suited for protecting people from deadly arrows. He had been ordered to be executed by

*A scene by Dürer shows men and women at prayer, reflecting personal piety.*

arrows for refusing, as a Roman soldier, to worship the Imperial cult. However, St Irene had cured his deadly wounds. As a result, he is portrayed as a figure bound to a tree pierced by many arrows. St Roch (d. 1327) was also a popular choice. Although St Sebastian was a well-known figure, St Roch was somewhat obscure, though more recent. He had dedicated himself to soothing the distress of the ill. In addition, he had a swelling on his left thigh that could be interpreted as a bubo; images of St Roch show him pulling up his clothing and pointing to the swelling.

First and foremost, those in fear of plague would have turned to the Virgin Mary. She was the greatest intercessor as the Mother of God. She was often portrayed sheltering souls under her cape as arrows fell upon them. Thus, not only was she likely to be able successfully to plead with her son for mercy, but she was also an active protector of the poor Christians against 'the slings and arrows of outrageous fortune'. Moreover, some statues of the Virgin focus on the grief she felt at the sufferings of her son and portray her as 'wounded' by lances, spears, swords and sometimes arrows. In all three intercessors, there are some recurring themes. For specific reasons it was felt that these individuals would understand the suffering of those facing plague. Also, both the Virgin and St Sebastian were associated with arrows in the pictures and statues of the churches. Thus, there was a natural conflation of the symbolism of plague as arrows of divine wrath and the ability to ward off, or recover from, arrows. This allegorical interpretation of the role of the Virgin and St Sebastian contrasts with the more 'obvious' appeal of St Roch. He had dedicated his life to helping the sick and had been afflicted by a swelling near his groin. Regardless of the reasoning behind the choice, the Virgin and Saints Sebastian and Roch became the focus for prayers seeking comfort, protection, release and intercession by individuals and communities beset by pestilence.

A more complex religious reaction was to rely on personal piety and devotion. Since the institutional structure of the Church

*Souls are punished for their sins in*
*the flames of purgatory.*

had seemingly failed (by dying or fleeing), people were forced to consider personal actions they might take for the care of their bodies and souls. Clearly, one could emphasise devotion to the Virgin or Saints Sebastian and Roch. One could also worship God more directly in private or in the home, as did the Brethren of the Common Life (a semi-monastic lay movement). Masses for the dead (who might well have died without last rites) became increasingly popular, as did an increasing awareness of the horrors of purgatory, where souls were 'purged' of sin before final admission into Heaven. Pilgrimages, on which one could earn grace, were a means of storing up the spiritual benefits, which might be of use during a plague or in purgatory. Mysticism and a focus on death, although they have their roots in trends before the Black Death, came to the fore. For example, the imagery of the Dance of Death (danse macabre, Totentanz) became more frequent (and gruesome). Funerary monuments began to stress decay and

*Two scenes from the Dance of Death sequence drawn by Hans Holbein in the early sixteenth century. Death accompanies the ploughman and torments the bishop.*

the horrors of the grave, rather than the resurrection and the afterlife.

To the modern mind, no response is more interesting or bizarre than that of the Flagellants. Before looking at them in detail, it is important to stress three major points. First, there were Flagellants in periods before the Black Death (for example, in the millennial fervour before the year 1000 and the 'Great Alleluia' of Italy in 1260) and in other religions (for example, in Shi'a Islam to the present day). Second, although a relatively common phenomenon, Flagellism was primarily a German response to plague and lasted for only a short while. Finally, the behaviour was very quickly (within a year) repudiated by State and Church and condemned outright by Pope Clement VI on 20 October 1349.

The simple explanation for the Flagellants is that they believed that by punishing their bodies they would appease God's wrath and He would remove the plague. Often, the Flagellants claimed that God had directly inspired their actions by a letter dropped from the sky. They moved from city to city in bands with their self-appointed leaders. Once in a city, they would surround a church and begin their ritual dance and penance while singing hymns. If anyone broke the circle, the process would have to begin again. At the end of the dance, they would all fall to the ground and then beat themselves. Their self-mutilation was recorded in the *Chronicon Henrici de Hervordia*:

> Each whip consisted of a stick with three knotted thongs hanging from the end. Two pieces of needle-sharp metal were run through the centre of the knots from both sides, forming a cross, the end of which extended beyond the knots for the length of a grain of wheat or less. Using these whips they beat and whipped their bare skin until their bodies were bruised and swollen and blood rained down, spattering the walls nearby. I have seen, when they whipped themselves, how sometimes those bits of metal penetrated the skin so deeply that it took more than two attempts to pull them out.

The writer also showed his disdain for the practice and official opposition when he reported that:

> However the flagellants ignored and scorned the sentence of excommunication pronounced against them by bishops. They took no notice of the papal order against them – until princes, nobles and the more powerful citizens started to keep them at a distance. The people of Osnabrück never let them in, although their wives and other women clamoured for them. Afterwards they disappeared as suddenly as they had come, as apparitions or ghosts are routed by mockery.

This mass bloodletting, although rejected by the clergy (who saw it as a threat to their monopoly on spiritual and intercessory power) and the secular rulers (who were frightened of mobs at the best of times), was nevertheless very popular. The theatrical value alone would have guaranteed an enormous crowd. More importantly, this act of bodily mortification was an act of devotion. So potentially powerful was it that reports said that 'some foolish women had clothes ready to catch the blood and smear it on their eyes, saying it was miraculous blood'.

One final mass movement is worth noting because it shows that such activities need not lead to the excesses of the Flagellants. In 1399, a rumour spread across Italy that the Virgin had appeared to a young shepherd. She said that her son, Christ, was angry with men for their sins and had already destroyed a third of the world as a punishment and warning. If something were not done, worse would undoubtedly follow. Although the apparition of the Virgin was said to have occurred in France, the only response was in Italy. In 1399, large groups of people moved across Italy dressed in white (for which they were called Bianchi). They sang hymns (as had the Flagellants) and did penance (though not of a violent kind). More dramatically, in the fractious milieu that was city-state Italy, they called for peace and demanded that warfare cease. Although the Church was not enthusiastic, it did give its blessing to these bands led by their self-appointed

*'The Dance of Death' from the* Nuremberg Chronicle.

leaders. Their appeal for peace ended – as does this recounting of the first half-century of plague – on a sad note: the outbreak of plague in 1400 was probably the worst since the Black Death.

❖         ❖         ❖

Readers may already have noted one puzzling feature in the foregoing discussion. There has been a conscious effort to use a range of words to describe the disease that struck the West in 1347. Indeed, the term 'Black Death' has been used sparingly. There are two primary reasons for this. The first relates to the phrase 'Black Death'. The term seems to have come into use in the mid-sixteenth century and only became common in English in the nineteenth century. It remains unfashionable among the historians of Italy, France and Spain to this day. At the time, Christians most often referred to the events of 1347-1351 as the 'Great Death' or the 'Great Pestilence'. Muslims had a greater, and more evocative, range of expressions: the Universal Plague, the Plague of the Kindred, the Great Destruction, the Great Plague, the Great Pestilence, and – most poignant of all – the Year of the Annihilation.

The more complex reasons for using epidemic, plague, and pestilence interchangeably relates to the identification of the disease itself. For most, the word plague denotes bubonic plague, while epidemic and pestilence are less specific terms. Although many will perhaps find this surprising, there still remains a serious debate among scholars as to the correct identification of the disease. In part, the problem arises from the sources surviving from the period. Chroniclers were not pathologists or diagnostic clinicians. They often fail to provide detailed information on the symptoms of the afflicted. Also, there is the possibility that they did not differentiate between deaths caused by the primary disease (plague) and secondary infections (for example, pneumonia). Moreover, since the disease disappeared in Europe after the early eighteenth century, there has not been a continuous historical and medical discussion of the disease as one finds with syphilis, measles or smallpox. Thus, there is the possibility that the disease clinically identified in the 1890s may not have been the disease that battered Europe in 1347-1722 or even during the First Pandemic.

The disease known as plague today was first identified scientifically with the isolation of the microbe in 1894. Alexandre Yersin, who had trained at the Pasteur Institute in Paris, rushed to Hong Kong in the midst of an epidemic. He isolated the bacillus and produced a serum. The cause of this Third Pandemic (1894-99) was named *Pasteurella pestis* (or, more commonly now, *Yersinia pestis*). The disease ravaged Hunan, Canton and Hong Kong before moving to the Bombay Presidency, the Bengal Presidency (including Calcutta), Oporto, Glasgow and Sydney. The disease presents itself in three distinct forms, each named after their most obvious characteristic: bubonic (buboes or swellings are present), septicemic (the bacillus is concentrated in the blood) and pneumonic (the bacillus accumulates in the lungs and is expelled in the sputum). The same bacillus causes each form and it is not actually known why the disease presents in the differing forms.

However, *Yersinia pestis* is not a human bacillus. Normally, it is found in rats and other rodents and is passed by their fleas from animal to animal. On occasion, the concentration of the bacillus can cause a massive mortality in the rodent population. When this occurs, the rodents' fleas will jump to any warm body. If there is a sufficient concentration of the bacillus in the flea, its sucking organ will become blocked and the bacillus will be expelled into the host. During periods of rodent mortality, their fleas can infest humans and transmit the bacillus to them. The black rat, long blamed for the epidemic, is thought a less likely candidate than the brown. The black rat, although rather gregarious, tends to live in the countryside, while the brown rat happily lives in close proximity to humans. However, since the brown rat has a very limited territory, it seems an unlikely candidate for a rapidly spreading epidemic. There has been some speculation that human fleas or lice may have helped perpetuate the disease in late antiquity and the Middle Ages. The assumption is that human fleas and lice, though infrequent carriers, infested humans in such quantities that they might well have managed to spread the infection once the disease had made the transition from rodents to humans.

Most scholars who identify the epidemic of 1347 with *Yersinia pestis* assume that the bubonic form was, by far, the most common form present. After a carrier flea bites a person, the bacillus incubates for two to eight days. Then the patient is struck with a high fever

(105°F) accompanied by convulsions, vomiting, giddiness, photo-sensitivity, and extreme pain in the limbs. The patient appears dazed and stupefied. Assuming the afflicted is strong, within two to three days of the onset of the fever, the lymph glands (in the groin, neck or armpits) nearest the bite begin to swell dramatically (from egg size to that of an apple). Eventually, these very painful swellings (buboes) will sweat and burst. In severe cases, livid, crimson spots (*petechiae*) appear on the skin. In 25-30 per cent of cases, recovery comes in eight to ten days. Those that die do so from exhaustion, heart failure or internal bleeding.

Although most believe that bubonic is the normative form of plague, some would argue that the pneumonic form was also present in the Black Death. Once the bacillus has incubated, instead of a high fever, the patient experiences a sharp drop in temperature. The bacillus retreats to the lungs, which fill with bacillus-laden fluid. The disease spreads through bloody sputum expelled by coughing, sneezing or even talking. Within days the patient evidences extreme neurological disorders and falls into a coma. This form is fatal in over 95 per cent of cases. Pneumonic is the only form of plague that can be transmitted from human to human without the intervention of an intermediary insect.

Septicemic plague is extremely rare, though always fatal. For some reason, the bacillus infests the blood after the person is bitten. The concentration in the blood stream produces a rash (from thousands of burst capillaries) within hours and death occurs within a day. Although extremely rare and unable to spread very effectively (the carrier dies too quickly), the concentration of the bacillus in the blood might allow the bacillus to be gathered and spread by human fleas and lice. Modern medicine has also identified two other even rarer variants: *Yersinia pseudo-tuberculosis* (which presents like tuberculosis) and *Yersinia enterocolita* (which infests the lower digestive tract).

One must compare these specifically identified medical diseases with what is known about the disease that afflicted Europe in

1347. Chroniclers then (and in subsequent outbreaks) mention swellings (often in the groins), fever, splotches (which are actually rare in bubonic plague) and delirium. Many of these symptoms are also present in other virulent diseases: anthrax, tuberculosis, typhoid and typhus. The greatest problem with an accurate identification of the pestilence with bubonic plague relates to its pattern of behaviour on the grand scale. For example, *Yersinia pestis* will only infect humans if the rodent fleas are forced to abandon their normal hosts. That is, any outbreak of plague among humans should be preceded by a massive mortality among the rodents. No such mortality is noted in Western chroniclers, although Chinese and Islamic sources do occasionally associate mass rodent deaths with the appearance of plague in humans.

If bubonic plague (that is, the disease isolated in 1894) is the culprit, then one must explain how it managed to move from city to city. Even with the 'milder' bubonic form, the incubation period of two to eight days would hardly seem likely to allow an infected person to get from one place to the next. And, even if he were to make it, bubonic plague cannot be transmitted from person to person. Rat fleas would not stay on humans that long either. Although the black rat might cover such distances, he is unlikely to come into intimate contact with humans. The brown rat lives in houses but rarely travels far. In other words, our knowledge of the modern *Yersinia pestis* does not correlate well with the facts from the Middle Ages.

A number of explanations have been given to explain these discrepancies. First, some have suggested that another disease altogether might be to blame (for example, anthrax). Others have suggested that the disease has mutated over time and, therefore, the bacillus of late antiquity and the Middle Ages was sufficiently different to account for the apparent discrepancies. This explanation was frequently dismissed as simply too convenient until the sudden appearance of the HIV/AIDS virus and the identification of the speed of mutation among antibiotic-resistant bacteria. Both viruses and bacteria now seem considerably more adaptable than was previously thought. Finally, some have theorised that the mutation lies not in the bacillus but in man. That is, the present population is, almost inevitably, descended from a genetic stock able to withstand the plague.

Although there is an almost irresistible fascination with this debate, in some ways it is pointless. There is no clinical way to identify the disease that ravaged Europe in either of the first two pandemics. In that sense, the debate can never be resolved. More importantly, the argument has had the tendency of obscuring the events themselves. Even if one could with certainty identify the disease, one would still be unsure how many died directly from it, rather than from secondary infections. Also, the exact name of the plague would not alter the events. Just as many people would remain dead, the responses would be no different: an appreciation for the impact and consequences of the plague – the telling of the history of the disease – is not dependent upon, or altered by, the exact clinical name given to the pestilence.

The reality is that the people of the past knew what disease was killing them and they had a name for it: plague/pestilence. They learned to react to that disease in specific ways. They understood what it was, when it would strike and what the consequences were likely to be. Western Europeans lived with this disease for nearly 400 years. For very logical reasons, specific to and dependent upon their view of reality, they were convinced that they could cope with the disease and, on occasion, ameliorate its effect. While superficially fascinating – and an ideal opportunity for academics to demonstrate their grasp of clinical medicine and pathology – the debate about the 'correct' identification of the disease simply serves to detract from an attempt to understand the impact of the disease and the responses to it.

*—◦ Three ◦—*

# DANCING WITH DEATH
## Understanding and Regulating Plague
### 1400–1500

*You must cure the causes of plague which are the horrendous sins being commit-
ted: blasphemy against God and the saints, the schools of sodomy, the outrageous
usury … Take action, take action and you will deal with the plague.*

Franciscan sermon

B y the end of the fourteenth century, it was fairly obvious
to everyone that plague had become a regular and
destructive aspect of life. The Black Death had proved not to be
one horrible catastrophe, but rather a shocking introduction to a
new and lasting menace. Death, in the form of this new pestilential
disease, danced across Europe on a cyclical basis, leaving devastated
communities in its wake. Although the plague seems to have left
many rural areas relatively untouched after the late 1300s, for
towns and cities, the epidemic returned almost every decade. The
first appearances of buboes in early summer, the rapid increase in
mortality, the collapse of normal life, the waning of the plague in
early winter – these events became as much a part of the normal
rhythm of life as the return of the seasons and the holy days of the
Church. Western society, especially its urban centres, was forced
to accept and adapt to the plague. Either ways had to be found to

prevent the arrival or mitigate the impact of the disease, or cities would not long survive. Unable to receive the plague with equanimity as a blessing from God as Islamic societies did, the Christian West strove to avert or appease His wrathful curse. This chapter will focus on the methods for preventing, containing and curing plague as they were developed in Italy during the course of the fifteenth century. For nearly three centuries, these ordinances and regulations formed the framework for coping with the pestilence throughout Western Europe.

These responses fell into three broad categories. First, governments attempted to control the spread of the disease through limitations on the movements of people and goods. Quarantines, health certificates and urban sanitation were some of the methods employed. There was also a general religious response that relied heavily on personal and communal piety, prayers, pilgrimages and processions. Finally, society as a body had methods for coping with the disease. These could include, as we have already seen, a devil-may-care attitude to life and, more disturbingly, the identification and persecution of scapegoats. It was possible to combine elements from each of these methodologies in any given outbreak of pestilence. For example, as will be discussed in greater detail below, the society could identify a group (Jews) as plague-bearers who would then be expelled or executed by the state and the entire event commemorated by the building of a church or shrine (on the site of the ghetto or, better, the synagogue). Indeed, the normal response to plague was to combine (or try) as many 'solutions' as possible.

When plague first appeared, the range of responses was fairly limited. In effect, the officials simply modified methods used for dealing with other epidemic diseases with which they were familiar. For example, when influenza struck, most urban areas would order that anything which smelled should be removed from the city. Thus, offal was collected, tanners and leather workers told to stop work or to ensure their by-products were quickly removed, and human waste was banned from the streets and gutters. If this failed to halt the disease then people who were considered morally contaminating were also removed. So, prostitutes, vagabonds, and other 'sinners' were chased from the city. These responses were based on the simple principle that disease was caused by an infection (miasma) in the general environment, meaning that the physical world could become polluted through bad smells or bad people. The best way to stop disease was to cleanse the city of pollution.

When plague struck these general methods were employed but to little effect. Moreover, it soon became apparent that an even greater danger confronted communities. During the very first occurrences of pestilence, some cities instituted temporary health committees or boards of leading citizens and magistrates. This, too, was in line with the normal practices used for other epidemic diseases. However, once the sheer scale of the danger associated with plague became obvious, leading figures in urban areas preferred to flee to rural areas before the disease actually broke out. This left cities without any leadership. As a result, looting became a serious danger. Magistrates feared that the common people and artisans might use a plague outbreak and the absence of their rulers to seize power. In the 1383 outbreak, Florentine artisans roamed around the city shouting revolutionary slogans, but the remaining magistrates were able to put down the nascent revolt and add to the general mortality by executing the leading malcontents. The city then attempted to prevent the flight of leading citizens but with little success as Marchionne Stefani, a contemporary chronicler, noted:

> Many laws were passed that no citizens could leave because of the said plague. For [the rulers] feared that the [common people] would not leave, and would rise, and the malcontents would unite them … [These laws failed because] it is always so that large and powerful beasts jump and break fences.

*Based on a fifteenth-century woodcut, this picture shows a plague patient being treated by a physician. The patent inability of medical practitioners to cure plague did not stop people from turning to them in desperation. Note the censer in the foreground, used to perfume the air and dispel evil odours.*

Thus, beyond preventing and containing disease, urban elites had to find some way to prevent chaos and contain their populations. Responding to plague became as much a matter of social control as disease management.

With no immediate means of explaining, preventing or eliminating disease being proffered by their secular rulers, people turned to their medical and religious advisers. The leading physicians explained that plagues appeared for a number of reasons. For example, a specific arrangement of heavenly bodies might cause a disturbance in the atmosphere (environment) resulting in a maismic (polluting and defiled) disturbance. These learned men were, first and foremost, philosophers. They theorised about disease utilising the philosophical presuppositions of the ancient thinkers (especially Aristotle) in combination with the philosophical and logic-based writings of ancient practitioners (especially Galen and, through his interpretations, Hippocrates). In opposition to this intellectual response to disease was the approach of the empirics, those who arrived at their interpretations of disease by experience and observation. Since the empirics used only observation and had no necessary training in the fine art of thinking, leading university-trained physicians considered them, and their methods and views, inferior. As a leading physician, Eleazer Dunk (writing in the early 1600s after two and a half centuries of plague) explained:

> The name of an Empirike … [means] experience; and by an Empirike is … [meant] a [medical] Practitioner, that hath no knowledge of Philosophy, Logicke, or Grammar; but fetcheth all his skill from bare and naked experience. Ignorance then is the difference whereby these men are distinguished from other Physicians.

*This English manuscript includes a number of spells and herbal remedies for diseases including, midway down this page, 'a drynke for pestylence'.*

Thus, the first thing that anyone learned when consulting a physician about the plague was that observation and experience were of no use in understanding, preventing, containing or elimitating it. Philosophy and ancient wisdom insisted on a particular set of presuppositions about reality and the logical conclusion from these was that plague was a type of fever caused by bad air.

These men might be useful in prescribing a moderate regime of diet, exercise and behaviour tending to promote general health, but they were wholly unable to deal with a contagious disease. Moreover, since they felt most, if not all, disease arose from environmental (or 'dispositional') factors there was little to do after disease erupted. Prevention was their forte. However, since certain geographical situations (for example, damp, swampy lands) and particular behavioural realities (for example, poverty or licentiousness) were by their very nature unhealthy, they could only suggest their elimination. This action might prevent the advent of an epidemic or, possibly, curtail its virulence.

The other possible source of advice during an epidemic was the clergy. Since they had a special relationship with the divine, it was possible that they might be able to explain or alter the course of an epidemic. Their explanation was considerably less cerebral than that of the physicians. There was an obvious reason for plague: God was angry with the community. It was absolutely essential that the sins that were inviting divine anger be identified and eliminated. Three key targets could be identified. First, the general piety or impiety of the entire community was examined. People were encouraged to avail themselves of the sacraments of the Church, to make pilgrimages, to pray, to participate in processions and to perform other pious acts. Second, the community might be guilty of harbouring impious and ungodly beliefs. Thus, heresy had to be rooted out and, coupled with this, the most obvious group of unorthodox, the Jews. Since the Jews rejected the 'truths' of the Christian faith they were seen as the enemies of God and, by extension, the followers of God's great enemy, Satan – as were

*Woodcuts illustrating two of the corporal acts of mercy: Christ looks on as a woman ministers to a prisoner (above) and buries the dead (below). Concern about personal piety was an important feature of the period.*

*Pilgrimages were another form of personal piety undertaken by those fearful of God's displeasure. In commissioning this illustration, John Stabius (whose arms are shown along with those of the Holy Roman Emperor, Austria and Scotland) sought to indicate his piety by being portrayed as the pilgrim St Coloman.*

heretics. Finally, societies were counselled to root out those sins that were most visible and likely to provoke God's wrath. Prostitution and same-sex acts were obvious targets.

In effect, the religious leaders were advising a similar course to that of the physicians. The problems that caused epidemic diseases were environmental. Something in the region was infecting the community. Physicians looked to pollution in the air in the natural sense, while religious leaders assumed that pollution was present (in the air) in a metaphorical and religious sense. To both, the plague was the result of factors already in existence in a locality and body politic. Plague was not 'caught' from someone or somewhere else. Plague 'broke out' because of the polluted conditions already present. Things, people and places did not carry and spread plague (by contagion) in a neutral sense. Rather, pestilence appeared because those factors that caused disease were already present. The way to prevent, curtail or cure plague, for both physicians and religious leaders, was to change those environmental aspects that were sources of pollution. While magistrates were willing to accept that bad sanitation might worsen civic health, they consistently held to the view that plague was a contagious disease, not a fever caused by bad air. In addition, they were also willing to believe that God's wrath might be kindled against a city in the form of a contagious epidemic. The common people were especially inclined to agree that specific acts (especially those of others) were to blame. Whatever the theoretical reasoning, one course of action was obvious: the community had to cleanse itself of pollution and prevent recontamination.

❖     ❖     ❖

Attacks against Jews were the most obvious and horrific example of this attempt to purify urban communities of groups and individuals considered polluting and diseased. By 1550, there were almost no Jews left in Western Europe, as country after country had expelled or executed their Jewish people. However, anti-Semitism did not start with the plague; Edward I (1239-1307) had expelled England's Jewish population in the 1290s. In 1215, the Fourth Lateran Ecumenical Council had ordered that all Jews and Muslims wear special clothes and distinguishing badges on their garments so that everyone would be able to identify them with ease and at a distance. The Council's requirement that belief in transubstantiation (that the bread and wine in communion actually become Christ's Body and Blood) was a necessary article of faith also became important in subsequent accusations against Jews for supposed attacks on the host. Throughout the thirteenth and fourteenth centuries, there had been increasingly strong attacks on Jews, especially (though not exclusively) in the preaching campaigns of the Dominicans and Franciscans. The appearance of plague and the accusation that Jews were intentionally spreading the pestilence combined to accelerate the calls of the friars for the complete expulsion of the Jews from the Christian West.

The accusations against the Jews were manifold. They were seen as the group solely responsible for the crucifixion of Christ, despite the involvement of Pilate and the Roman (that is, Gentile) Empire. In addition, rumours asserted that Jews used the blood of Christian children (called the Blood Libel) in various religious ceremonies (for example, Passover). Their enemies accused them of stealing consecrated hosts (Host Desecration) for similar uses. Jews were frequently accused of conspiring with Muslims and heretical or Orthodox Christians against western Catholics. Also, there were accusations that the seeming stubbornness of the Jews in refusing to accept the 'truth' of Christianity was a further sign of their intentional and conscious evil, which inevitably led to associating them with Satan and demonic practices. Even accuasations of arson attacks and other catastrophic events were laid at their doors. Finally, during the plague outbreaks of the late fourteenth and early fifteenth centuries, the Jews were accused of working with, in turn, Muslims, lepers and the Devil to poison wells and spread the plague. Many leading churchmen condemned these attacks following the teaching of St Augustine of Hippo (354-430) that Jews must be tolerated as an essential part of the cosmic history of Christendom. Indeed, Pope Clement VI and subsequent Popes all condemned attempts to blame Jews for the plague – they noted that Jews and Christians seemed to be dying in equal numbers from the pestilence.

As early as the 1100s, a Christian chronicler noted the impact of popular anti-Semitism and wrote that 'whether what I am relating is true or not is no concern of mine; it is told thus and thus must it be accepted'. In the decade immediately before the plague (1337), parishioners in Deggendorf (Bavaria) dedicated a plaque on a church commemorating the fact that 'here were the Jews slain; they had set the city afire'. Other churches were raised as memorials to the destruction of Jewish quarters (ghettos) and especially synagogues. In 1300, at Lauda (Würzburg), a massacre accompanying an accusation of Host Desecration saw a chapel built on the site of the demolished Jewish houses. Indeed, many of the churches dating from this period that are dedicated to the Body of Christ (Corpus Christi), the Holy Blood, or the Virgin Mary stand on ground formerly occupied by Jewish homes or places of worship.

Plague simply seems to have accelerated and intensified the persecution – and elimination – of Jews. In the 1340s, Jews were targeted as plague-bringers in France, Italy, Switzerland and Germany. Some citizens even cleansed their cities of Jews before the arrival of plague in an attempt to prevent the pestilence; such preventative persecution appeared at Strasbourg (900 Jews were burned alive), Nuremburg, Regensburg, Augsburg and Frankfurt. The Holy Roman Emperor, Charles IV (1316-78), even made laws arranging for the disposal of Jewish property in the event of the elimination of a ghetto. The persecution of Jews remained a consistent feature accompanying many plague outbreaks: Halle (1382); Rappoltsweiler, Dürkheim, Colmar (1397); Freiburg-im-Breisgau (1401); Cologne (1424); Schweidnitz (1448-53, 1543); Regensburg (1472); Germany-wide (1475); Brieg (1541); Aix-en-Provence (1580); and Vienna (1679). Pre-existing accusations of well-poisoning seem to explain this association of Jews with plague. As early as 877, a Jewish doctor was accused of poisoning Emperor Charles the Bold (823-77); in 1161, eighty-six Jews were executed in a single massacre as poisoners. Jews, along with Muslims and lepers, were subsequently accused of poisoning in the Vaud (1308); Eulenburg (1316); Franconia (1319); France-wide (1321); Provence, Germany-wide (1337); and Provence (1348). The move from persecution for poisoning to persecution for plague-spreading was virtually seamless.

There also seems to have been a connection between these accusations for poisoning and plague-spreading with the involvement of Jews in medical work. The emphasis upon literacy among Jews, as well as their prohibition from many trades (especially farming and land-ownership), meant that Jews were concentrated in urban areas and over-represented in professions that required the ability to read. In addition, Jewish familiarity with Hebrew and Arabic gave many Jews access to the medical works of the ancients through the medium of the Islamic world. Indeed, Jewish medical skills often allowed them to work in areas otherwise closed to their co-religionists. For example, despite the expulsion of Jews from England by Edward I, both Edward II (1284-1327) and Henry IV (1367-1413) employed Jews as personal physicians (a practice quite common among many noble and wealthy families). The power of Jewish physicians was a frequent concern to many. In the sixteenth century, Hans Wilhelm Kirchhoff noted that 'we Christians are such brainless fools that when our lives are in danger we turn to our arch-enemies [the Jews] in order to save [ourselves]'. The friars were especially keen to stop this reliance on Jewish medical practitioners and were so successful that many Italian cities were forced to get explicit Papal permission (dispensation) to employ Jews as civic physicians.

The complex interaction between Jews as healers and as poisoners is obvious. Although Jews were clearly outsiders and suspect, they were also essential to certain areas of life. Only with an increase in gentile (Christian) involvement in medicine and finance (to name but two areas) was it possible to survive without a dependence upon Jews. However, a reliance on Jews in no way altered the overwhelmingly negative and suspicious image of them in the minds of most, if not all, Christians. As Peter the Venerable (1122-57), Abbot of Cluny, put it: 'really I doubt whether a Jew can be human for he will neither yield to human reasoning [and accept Christianity], nor find satisfaction in authoritative utterances, alike divine and Jewish [in refusing to accept the Catholic interpretation of the books of the Jewish/Old Testament]'. Shakespeare (*Merchant of Venice* II.ii.27) penned a more succinct and blunt assessment: 'Certainly the Jew is the very devil incarnal'.

While Jews were more easily identifiable, they were not the only groups in a society to be attacked after being blamed for causing a pestilential outbreak. Poor foreigners (those who would be called 'economic migrants' today) were usually expelled at the merest hint of plague. Refugees from wars and persecution (today's 'asylum seekers') were often seen as 'dirty' and, therefore, a potential source of disease. Tanners, leather-makers, butchers, fishmongers and gravediggers, whose professions produced bad smells or refuse, often saw their labours curtailed during plague outbreaks. Consistently, though, the emphasis was placed upon controlling any group or individual who was associated with dirt, pollution, refuse and illness. People involved in the sex trade or sexual deviance were, unsurprisingly, targeted as often as Jews and, after the expulsion of most of Europe's Jews, one of the few groups of potential scapegoats remaining.

❖      ❖      ❖

It is essential to realise that attitudes to sex and sexuality in the late medieval period differ quite dramatically from those of today. For example, until very late in the fifteenth century (and often until a century later) brothels remained an accepted – and legal – part of the civic landscape. Brothels were built with public funds and overseen by a state-appointed or state-approved 'madam' (often called the 'abbess' or 'queen of whores'). Thus, in 1447, Dijon constructed a substantial building to serve as the city's brothel. There were rooms for the custodian, a spacious common room and nearly two dozen large bedrooms, each with a stone fireplace. This city of 10,000 souls was well provided for with over a hundred legally recognised prostitutes.

Many publicly maintained bathhouses were used for prostitution and there were also small, 'private' brothels. Most of these establishments and activities were openly recognised, regulated and taxed by the city government. In addition to this licit activity, there were streetwalkers. The magistrates justified the provision of pros-

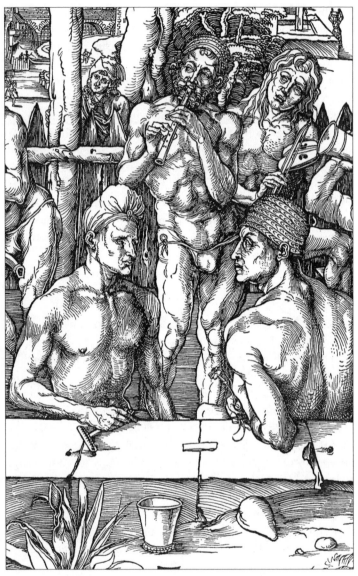

*An engraving by Dürer from the late fifteenth century showing men at the bathhouse.*

titutes (to their often-censorious clergy) on the grounds of 'common utility' and '[being] in the interest of the public good'. They were meant to provide an outlet for the sexual appetites of the many single young men. Since artisans and workers were not usually allowed to marry until they became masters of their trade (that is, in their thirties), young men were a serious problem. Prostitutes were seen as an acceptable alternative to the gang raping of 'respectable' young women or men in the street, which happened not infrequently. In addition to providing societies with money (through taxes) and order (through the release of sexual tension), legal prostitution gave the city the chance to ensure that the sex-workers and the brothels were 'clean'.

Initially, there seems to have been no clear identification of legal prostitution (in brothels) with plague. Indeed, 1350-1450 was the period of the construction and institutionalisation of public brothels. Rather than removing the sex-workers, the city governments seem to have been concerned to ensure that they were clean. The preaching friars, however, stressed that physical cleanliness and health were no cover for the moral dirtiness of the activity. They went further and asserted that legalisation inextricably tied the society, in general, with an unwholesome activity. The general populace seems to have agreed and prostitutes (who, like Jews, were often required to wear distinctive badges or clothes) were attacked in time of plague or harvest failure or after especially successful and charismatic sermons. Still, until the 1480s, most single men went to brothels as a regular feature of their Sunday life – the brothels were only required to close during the actual time of the main Mass. In the later decades of the fifteenth century, prostitution came under increasing attack by preachers and, especially during the Protestant and Catholic Reformations of the sixteenth century, by society in general.

It is perhaps difficult today to understand how the preachers were able to convince society that legal prostitution was so dangerous. Most men would, at some time prior to marriage, have visited brothels. Fathers sent their sons to them quite openly. Shame was not an effective tool. However, the preachers were able to accuse the society of supporting a behaviour that was unable to restore the population of Europe constantly devastated by plague. That is, prostitution (and illegitimacy) was unproductive and, therefore, sinful. As such, it was unnatural. This theoretical approach to sexual sins is most evident in the accompanying attack on same-sex acts. Male homosexuality (normally grouped under the general term of sodomy) was an equally unproductive activity and thus denounced by the preachers – lesbian acts seem rarely to have been noticed. The depopulation of Europe as a result of the plague put a great emphasis on the production of legitimate children. Future workers (children) were needed to restore society and anything that worked against this was a social evil. The preachers now had a way of making the sinfulness of prostitutes (fornicators and adulterers) and sodomites understandable to the common folk. These sins were not just an affront against God but also a threat to society and likely to invite further divine wrath. As St Bernardino (1380-1444) preached to his fellow citizens of Siena: 'you don't understand that [sodomy] is the reason you have lost half your population over the last twenty-five years'. He claimed that God's (poetic) judgement against a society that seemed to despise children (by refusing to have legitimate offspring) was to deprive the people of the few children they did bother to produce. He claimed that he could hear, ringing in his ears, the unborn (unconceived) chanting for vengeance.

It is not surprising that population loss was a major concern for civic governments and their populations. For example, in the 1330s, Florence comprised around 120,000 people. The population finally stabilised in 1410-60 at 40,000. Moral rectitude and duty to the wider society became matters of the utmost concern to the state. Florence made attempts to control political views (1378), street-walking (1403), sexual immorality in convents (1421), malfeasance in officials (1429) and sodomy (1432). The creation of the Ufficiali di Notte (Office of the Night) in 1432 to control sodomy led to seventy years of magisterial prosecution of men engaged in sex with other men (usually an older man with a younger). A similar institution (the Collegium sodomitarum) was established in Venice in 1418.

In the period 1432-1502, over 17,000 men (240 per year, nearly five each week) were accused and 3,000 (forty-three per year) were convicted of sodomy in a Florentine population of 40,000. If one takes a generation to be twenty years then in any generation about 12 per cent of the male population was publicly and official-ly accused of sodomy and 2 per cent actually convicted. The problem, it would seem, was not insignificant. The Florentine state even attempted to require that all magistrates aged from thirty to fifty had to be married to avoid any secret sodomites from working in the courts to protect others like themselves. So common was the practice that Bernardino accused fathers and mothers of knowingly allowing their sons to engage in same-sex acts and rela-tionships. He said that their sons should be locked up at home lest they be enticed into this behaviour. The saint preached that it was 'less evil' that their daughters be raped than their sons. He called sodomy 'this pestilential ruin' besetting the city. So close is the inter-relationship of sodomy, plague, pollution and sin that most Florentine laws and Bernardine sermons against sodomy occurred during or shortly after plague outbreaks.

What offended Bernardino and others the most, though, was the toleration of these sins at the highest levels of society. Nobles and the wealthy protected Jews for financial and medical reasons. Society's leaders legalised and protected prostitution. Worse still, many of the greatest figures in western Christian culture engaged in, or over-looked, sodomitical practices. For example, Poliziano (1454-1494) who was a tutor to the children of Lorenzo de' Medici (1449-92) and a friend and teacher of Michelangelo (1475-1564) – and a fur-ther 500 men from all over Europe – was a leading Neoplatonist figure of the Renaissance. He was also, to use the contemporary term, a 'notorious sodomite' who never married. He, and others, wrote poems about their love of other men. For example:

> If you would share in my society,
> Do not discourse on female love to me…
> I urge all husbands: seek divorce, and flee
> Each one away from female company

Cellini (1500-71), in August 1545, while talking to the Duke of Florence, was attacked by an opposing artist, Baccio: 'Oh keep quiet, you dirty sodomite'. Stunned by this public accusation, Cellini amused, but did not shock, the gathered courtiers when he replied:

> You madman, you're going too far. But I wish to God I did know how to indulge in such a noble practice [sodomy] … it is the practice of the greatest emperors and the greatest kings of the world. I'm an insignificant humble man, I haven't the means or the knowledge to meddle in such a marvellous manner.

His four arrests and two convictions for sodomy make his riposte all the more pithy.

It is hardly surprising that the Church and its clergy often attacked sodomy not only as a great sin but also as an extreme threat to the survival of society itself. However, the celibate clergy were not exempt from this infection. On 1 November 1494, Savonarola (1453-98) demanded of his fellow Florentine clerics that they 'abandon, I say, that unspeakable vice, abandon that abominable vice that has brought God's wrath upon you, or else: woe, woe to you!' In the end, the Council of Trent (1545-1563) was forced to attempt to outlaw pagan mythology and nudity – in 1559, draperies were painted on Michelangelo's nudes in the Sistine Chapel. Preachers, moralists and, increasingly, magistrates became convinced that immorality (social and cultural pollution) had to be eliminated. Clearly, they could not eradicate prostitution or sodomy any more than foreigners or refugee poor could be stopped at the border. However, society had to be seen by God to be trying to purify itself if divine punishment was to be avoided. During the course of the fifteenth century, it became clear to many that the 'toleration' of sinfulness and moral impurity was the cause of God's anger. To prevent epidemic diseases being sent against a society, it was essential that everything possible be done to eliminate the causes of pollution and defilement in the culture.

The general populace, with its clergy and magistrates, could take comfort in seeing prostitutes, sodomites, migrants, and the foreign poor driven from their streets and out of sight. Surely a society that moved harshly and strenuously against these sources of metaphorical, metaphysical and religious infection was less likely to suffer God's wrath. Lucy Hutchinson, in her diary of the early seventeenth century, could have spoken for most.

> The face of the court was much changed in the change of the King, for King Charles [I] was temperate, chaste, and serious; so that the fools and bawds, mimics and catamites [sodomites] of the former court [of James VI and I] grew out of fashion; and the nobility and courtiers, who did not quite abandon their debaucheries, yet so reverenced [feared] the king as to retire into corners to practice them.

Any society, cleansed of such vile pollution, could join her in breathing a collective sigh of relief.

❖       ❖       ❖

By the mid-fifteenth century, cities in northern Italy were taking a more practical approach to dealing with ill health and the threat of disease. Leaders of these city-states increasingly saw that they had a moral obligation to their societies as a whole. The state began to be seen as an organic whole with the rulers at the head. Instead of fleeing their posts before or during a plague, they had a civic responsibility to remain and control the situation. Maintaining social order and cohesion in the face of an epidemic became crucial. Since the physicians were unable to provide a cure, it was the duty of the leaders to ensure that the body politic would survive the pestilence. Controlling and managing people and the society were the important factors in developing the methods and practices adopted during plague. These regulations, ordinances and methodologies were developed in the city-states of northern Italy and from there spread throughout Western Europe.

One of the first things noticed by these magistrates was that plague behaved in a quite clear fashion. They came to the conclusion that the disease was contagious and could be carried by people and goods. Moreover, they concluded that the poor were more likely to contract – and, therefore, carry – the pestilence. While their trained physicians may have had little time for observation and experience, the magistrates involved in maintaining public health had no such prejudices against empirical analysis. Sadly, their interpretation of plague's causes and progress was no less tainted by theoretical presuppositions than those of the physicians. Rather, one might argue than these Italian regulations were never actually designed to cure plague. Instead they were intended, if possible, to slow the progress of the disease and, at all cost, to ensure that a stable society could survive an epidemic outbreak. Prevention, containment and survival took precedence over any possible curative. Order had to be maintained by the State while society endured the plague.

The first line of defence and the mainstay of these Italian regulations was controlling the movement of people and goods from an infected area into a region not yet struck by plague. This required a number of innovations. First, states that normally would have been quite secretive were forced to trust one another to announce when and where plague was present. This meant that governments had to stay in touch with one another and, even during times of war, cooperate in identifying plague-infected regions. Regular diplomacy and correspondence became an essential part of building the trust needed to allow cities to believe that statements about health were, in fact, truthful. When rumours of plague spread, the areas implicated were expected to certify if plague was present and notify their neighbours. These cities were then supposed to inform other adjacent states. The result was a frenzy of letter writing and, at times, visits by other magistrates and health officials.

In addition to identifying locales beset by plague, individuals were expected to present health certificates upon reaching a new town or city. These passports were granted by the places they had last visited and, in theory, guaranteed that the bearers – and goods – were not infected by plague nor had they been anywhere with the disease. Clearly, this required reliance, again, on the truthfulness and trustworthiness of other localities. It also meant that cities had to be more vigilant at their gates and invest in someone to read the passes. The bureaucracy required to maintain this system of passes was a tremendous burden on any state and was dependent upon a well-developed magistracy and civil service.

Since it was not always possible to trust one's neighbours, many cities introduced an extensive system of quarantine. Individuals and their goods trying to enter a city were frequently required to spend some period of time under observation at some distance from the town itself. Thus, ships might be asked initially to dock at an island off the coast rather than at the city's main quayside. Goods and merchants coming overland were likewise forced to wait before entering the gates. If those under quarantine possessed health certificates or passports attesting to their 'cleanliness' then they might only be confined for seven to twenty days. If they had been in or near an area infected with plague the quarantine might last forty days. Again, this system forced the state to invest heavily in personnel and structures. The quarantine areas had to be provided with medical practitioners to certify that their charges were plague-free. They also needed access to food, water and other provisions. Moreover, housing had to be available. Servants were needed to help the medical workers and supply the needs of the quarantined.

The prevention of plague's entry was extremely expensive and labour intensive. Every level required magisterial oversight even more so during the threat of plague. Full-time medical workers had to be employed to examine those trying to enter the city. Records had to be kept by literate servants. Heralds had to be employed to carry the correspondence between cities, and magistrates were sometimes forced to travel to areas rumoured to have plague to ensure themselves that the disease was not present. At every level, the first part of the Italian regulations required enormous sums of money, numerous personnel and constant magisterial supervision. The state bureaucracy had to become more efficient and more organised to meet the demands placed upon it.

The second aspect of the regulations related to identifying an outbreak of plague. Most Italian cities introduced legislation that required that all deaths be reported to the state. In addition, sudden deaths often had to be certified as unrelated to plague by official medical workers and magistrates. The most sophisticated cities demanded that a cause be noted for each death. Again, copious lists had to be kept. When plague was present, this system of identification altered to allow the state to differentiate plague dead from those who had died from other causes. Since infected corpses were thought contagious, it was essential that they be segregated from other bodies and disposed of at some distance from the city. This meant that plague dead could not be buried in local parish churches but should instead be interred outside the city's walls. Medical workers were, therefore, forced to visit the dead and dying even in the height of a plague outbreak, and families had to await an official verdict before being allowed to bury their dead. In the event of a plague death, the body was normally collected by special workers and buried in a deep mass grave. Clothing and other perishables associated with the corpse had to be destroyed.

There was a more devastating consequence for the family of a dead person if plague was identified. Not only was the body denied a normal burial, but the family was also quarantined. During the early stages of an outbreak, infected families might be sealed into their homes. Alternatively, where the facilities existed, these potentially contagious people might be forced to move either to a pest house or to temporary shelters placed outside the walls near the plague hospital. Subsequently, their linens and other perishable goods might be ordered destroyed or the entire house cleaned and fumigated. In either case, families were forced to endure the indignity of having their belongings rifled through (and perhaps pilfered) by poor plague workers. For most, this sequestration was a death sentence. As with the other aspects of these regulations, the confinement of families required a large number of workers, medical practitioners and, finally, magistrates to oversee and control the entire process.

Finally, the state was forced to sustain the people who were denied the right to support themselves. Those confined in their houses, plague hospitals or temporary cabins needed to be fed. The majority of those in quarantine were unlikely to have sufficient funds to care for themselves. This meant that the State had to collect enough in taxes to feed an increasingly large part of its population that was no longer able to work or pay these taxes. Also, since the workers in some trades (for example, tanners and butchers) were forced to curtail or suspend their labours, they had to be supported by the State, too. It was perfectly conceivable that during a plague outbreak the overwhelming majority of taxpayers would be unable to work. One of the most difficult tasks in these regulations guaranteeing order was the collection of taxes. The first responsibility of any health board attempting to assert its power and maintain order was to provide enough money and sufficient workers and magistrates to operate the system and care for the afflicted. It is perhaps understandable that a Palermo health official in 1576 said his motto was 'Gold, Fire and the Gallows'. Gold was needed to pay for the extensive and expensive regulations, fire was used to destroy infected goods, and the gallows stood as a constant

*Scenes demonstrating the measures taken to deal with the plague in Rome in 1656. The measures reflect those of the Italian states during the fifteenth century.*
Top: *Palaces and houses are shut up and the dead and dying are removed.*
Centre: *Plague regulations are publicly displayed for people to read.*
Bottom: *A surgeon, a priest and a physician stand by while the contents of an infected house are burnt.*

reminder of what would happen to anyone daring to disobey the authority of the health board.

The implementation of these regulations required the overcoming of a number of serious difficulties. First, the sheer level of organisation needed was tremendous. Most large states were unable to exert authority on this micro level. Only city-states seem to have been able to control their societies so closely. As a result, most large monarchical states (for example, France and England) were very late in implementing these regulations, while understanding their value. There was also an immense cost to these ordinances. The cost, though, was in more than mere money. Workers, trained medical practitioners and dedicated magistrates were needed to make the system work and they demanded substantial budgets. Finally, the greatest threat faced by states trying to impose the full range of Italian regulations (even in Italy) was the almost total unwillingness of the people to submit to them.

The common people were more than willing to accept that certain groups were the cause of plague. They needed no convincing that (moral) filthiness was a grave threat and had to be stamped out. After all, even today's children would know the aphorism that 'cleanliness is next to godliness'. What they resented was the attempt by the state to control their lives and to make them pay for the privilege. Every aspect of the regulations interfered with private commerce and private life. People, especially the poor, did not want the State visiting their houses to examine their dead or dying relations. They did not want their shops closed. They did not want to be sealed inside their houses or in distant fields and forced to depend on magisterial charity and organisation to supply their wants. If experience had taught the magistrates that the physicians and doctors were unable to prevent or cure plague, then the same experience had taught most poor people that these regulations were more likely to kill them than protect them. Moreover, they realised that this massive extension of official oversight into their lives and businesses would greatly restrict their activities and traditional liberties.

For their part, authorities in Italy very quickly made their temporary health boards permanent. The bureaucracy of the state gave the officials much greater control and more detailed information on their populations. The costs were indeed high and the situation difficult, but the returns were worth the effort. While the magistrates did hope to prevent plague's arrival and mitigate its effect once the epidemic broke out, the greater concern was that the society would survive the pestilence as a stable and orderly unit. The body politic (which supplied their needs at its head) had to be maintained. As a result of these ordinances, late medieval and early modern states appear increasingly 'modern'. Health inspectorates were created. Industries were inspected. Deaths were recorded. Burials were registered. Merchandise was certified. Passports were issued. From birth to death, the State now began to inspect, record and control many aspects of ordinary life. Plague was not regulated, but society was; health became an excuse for order.

# Four

# THE CIRCLE OF DEATH
## Endemic Plague
### 1500–1700

*Our prognosis [in plague cases] will be death rather than recovery as the disease is malignant, treacherous, pestiferous, and inimical to our vital spirits.*

Dr Parisi

n theory, by 1500, Western Europe had a well-established methodology for preventing and controlling plague outbreaks available in the systems developed in northern Italy's city-states. Sadly, as the previous chapter has shown, these regulations were much better at preventing and controlling social disorder. More importantly, two factors affected the continuing impact of plague on societies. First, most states (even those in northern Italy) were very slow to implement the entire range of plague regulations. Primarily, this was because of the immense costs and complex bureaucratic structures required for these ordinances.

Secondly, the whole cycle of plague altered dramatically. For the first 130 years (1347–c.1480) plague outbreaks recurred in most urban localities every six to twelve years. For most people this meant at least two to four outbreaks in one lifetime. However, around 1480 a significant change occurred. Thereafter, plague returned every fifteen to twenty years, or maybe only once or twice in any lifetime. Although less frequent, plague seems not to have become less virulent. Thus, just as Europe was developing methods for preserving its social structures and urban communities during and after plague attacks, the plague was becoming less threatening. City populations were better able to recover during the intervening years. In addition, the increasing focus of outbreaks on urban areas – and especially the urban poor – made it some-what easier to target regulations. Flight was certainly able to spread plague to rural areas but, on the whole, plague became understood primarily as an epidemic of a city's lower classes. However, since the disease was no less virulent, the dread of an outbreak did not lessen nor did the socio-cultural impetus for firm governmental action. Cities continued to need the protective application of the social 'medicine' of regulation, while hating the taste – and doubt-ing the efficacy – of the prescription.

Ironically, this alteration in the nature and pattern of pestilential outbreaks, coupled with the increasing popularity of Italian-style regulations, meant that states were busily trying to prevent a disease that was becoming less dangerous. However, the impetus for the implementation of the plague rules was, as has been frequently mentioned, primarily a function of social control. No matter how frequently – or infrequently – plague occurred, the impact was the same: cities almost collapsed as economic, social and political units. It was an essential element of State policy that the economic, social and political engines of early modern states (the cities) be protected and maintained. Anything that might limit the impact of a plague or speed the recovery of a city was attractive, since a disrupted city meant, in particular, the collapse of trade. No matter how reduced in real size (population), national governments wanted to ensure that the civic body politic (the city as a socio-economic and politi-cal unit) would emerge after a plague outbreak intact and functioning. In effect, what the Italian plague regulations were actually meant to obviate or eliminate were the dramatic economic and social consequences of plague. No one wanted to see a repeat of the dramatic changes that had occurred during the first half-century of the epidemic. Plague might have a tremendous immediate impact in terms of a high mortality rate, but more frightening was the possibility that it would usher in extensive change and alteration to the socio-political and economic realities of a state.

By the end of the period under consideration (*c.*1700), it was a European commonplace that Italy was 'the strictest place in the world, in the case of health', while England was considered one of the most backward states. However, the fame of Italy was won slowly since the articulation of ideas and theoretical rules was a long way from their actual adoption. The keystone of these health regulations was the establishment of health boards. Although many states were willing to set up temporary committees with extensive executive powers during the crisis of a plague outbreak, it was somewhat harder to convince societies (and traditional councils) to create new permanent bodies with wide-ranging powers in the areas of health and sanitation. It hardly took a brilliant magistrate to realise that any ambitious health board could, and probably would, manage to find a reason to meddle in almost every aspect of a society under the guise of health and sanitation. Thus, while Milan was quick to establish a permanent board before 1450, Venice did not follow until 1486, Florence until 1527 and Lucca until 1549. By 1600, though, even smaller towns and villages in Italy had boards or officers who were permanently responsible for the control of medical practitioners, the care of the sick and the running of the health institutions (hospices, workhouses and orphanages).

The extensive, expensive and literate bureaucracy required for the massive collection and collation of health-related information was also created slowly. For example, the need to identify the cause of deaths and to compile statistical information on the number of deaths categorised by cause was an important part of the regulatory system. To control health, the magistracy (especially in the form of the health board) needed reliable information on the state of the society. Again, Milan led the way by bringing in *Bills of Mortality*

# A generall Bill for this present year,

ending the 19 of *December* 1665 according to
the Report made to the KINGS most Excellent Majesty.

By the Company of Parish Clerks of *London*, &c.

| | buried. Pla. | | buried Pla. | | buried Pla. | | buried Pla. |
|---|---|---|---|---|---|---|---|
| St Albans Woodstreet | 200 | 121 | St Clements Eastcheap | 38 | 20 | St Margaret Moses | 38 | 25 | St Michael Cornehill | 104 | 52 |
| St Alhallowes Barking | 514 | 330 | St Dionis Back-church | 78 | 27 | St Margar. New Fishstr. | 114 | 66 | St Michael Crookedln. | 179 | 133 |
| St Alhallowes Breadft | 35 | 16 | St Dunstans East | 665 | 150 | St Margaret Pattens | 49 | 24 | St Mother. Queenehith | 203 | 122 |
| St Alhallowes Great | 455 | 426 | St Edmunds Lumbard | 70 | 26 | St Mary Abchurch | 99 | 54 | St Michael Querne | 44 | 18 |
| St Alhallowes Honilan | 10 | 5 | St Ethelborough | 105 | 106 | St Mary Aldermanbury | 181 | 109 | St Michael Royall | 152 | 116 |
| St Alhallowes Lesse | 239 | 175 | St Faiths | 104 | 70 | St Mary Aldermary | 105 | 75 | St Michael Woodstreet | 122 | 62 |
| St Alhall. Lumbardstr | 90 | 61 | St Fosters | 144 | 105 | St Mary le Bow | 64 | 26 | St Mildred Breadstreet | 59 | 26 |
| St Alhallowes Staining | 185 | 112 | St Gabriel Fen-church | 69 | 39 | St Mary Bothaw | 55 | 30 | St Mildred Poultrey | 68 | 46 |
| St Alhall. wee the Wall | 500 | 356 | St George Botolphlane | 41 | 27 | St Mary Colechurch | 17 | 6 | St Nicholas Acons | 46 | 18 |
| St Alphage | 270 | 115 | St Gregories by Pauls | 376 | 235 | St Mary Hill | 94 | 64 | St Nicholas Coleabby | 125 | 91 |
| St Andrew Hubbard | 71 | 25 | St Hellens | 108 | 75 | St Mary Mounthaw | 56 | 37 | St Nicholas Olaves | 90 | 62 |
| St Andrew Vndershaft | 274 | 189 | St James Dukes place | 163 | 190 | St Mary Summerset | 342 | 263 | St Olaves Hart-streete | 237 | 130 |
| St Andrew Wardrobe | 476 | 208 | St James Garlickhithe | 189 | 118 | St Mary Stainings | 47 | 27 | St Olaves Jewry | 54 | 32 |
| St Anne Alderfgate | 282 | 197 | St John Baptist | 128 | 83 | St Mary Woolchurch | 65 | 33 | St Olaves Silverstreet | 250 | 122 |
| St Anne Blacke-Friers | 652 | 467 | St John Euangelift | 9 | | St Mary Woolnoth | 75 | 38 | St Pancras Soperlane | 30 | 13 |
| St Antholins Parish | 58 | | St John Zacharie | 85 | 54 | St Martins Ironmonger. | 21 | 11 | St Peters Cheape | 62 | 35 |
| St Austins Parish | 43 | 20 | St Katherine Coleman | 299 | 213 | St Martins Ludgate | 196 | 128 | St Peters Cornc-hill | 136 | 76 |
| St Barthol. Exchange | 73 | 51 | St Katherine Creechu | 335 | 231 | St Martins Orgars | 110 | 71 | St Peters Pauls Wharfe | 114 | 86 |
| St Bennet Fynch | 47 | 23 | St Lawrence Jewrie | 94 | 48 | St Martins Outwitch | 70 | 34 | St Peters Poore | 79 | 47 |
| St Bennet Grace-chu | 57 | 41 | St Lawrence Pountney | 214 | 140 | St Martins Vintrey | 417 | 349 | St Stevens Coleman st | 560 | 391 |
| St Bennet Pauls Wharf | 355 | 172 | St Leonard Eastcheape | 42 | 27 | St Matthew Fridaystr. | 24 | 6 | St Stevens Walbrooke | 54 | 17 |
| St Bennet Sheerehog | 11 | 1 | St Leonard Fosterlane | 335 | 255 | St Maudlins Milkstree. | 44 | 22 | St Swithins | 93 | 56 |
| St Botolph Billingsgate | 85 | 50 | St Magnus Parish | 103 | 60 | St Maudlins Oldfishstr. | 176 | 121 | St Thomas Apostle | 163 | 110 |
| Christs Church | 653 | 467 | St Margaret Lothbury | 100 | 66 | St Michael Basfishaw | 253 | 164 | Trinitie Parish | 115 | 79 |
| St Christophers | 60 | 47 | | | | | | | | | |

Buried in the 97 Parishes within the walls, — 15207    Whereof, of the Plague — 9887

| | | | | | | | | |
|---|---|---|---|---|---|---|---|---|
| St Andrew Holborne | 3958 | 3103 | Bridewell Precinct | 230 | 179 | St Dunstans West | 958 | 665 | St Saviours Southwark | 4235 | 3446 |
| St Bartholomew Great | 493 | 344 | St Botolph Alderfgate | 997 | 755 | St George Southwark | 1613 | 1260 | St Sepulchres Parish | 4509 | 2746 |
| St Bartholomew Lesse | 193 | 139 | St Botolph Algate | 4926 | 4051 | St Giles Cripplegate | 8069 | 4838 | St Thomas Southwark | 475 | 371 |
| St Bridget | 2111 | 1427 | St Botolph Bishopsgate | 3464 | 2500 | St Olaves Southwark | 4793 | 2785 | Trinity Minories | 156 | 122 |
| | | | | | | | | | At the Pesthouse | 159 | 156 |

Buried in the 16 Parishes without of Walls — 41351    Whereof, of the Plague — 28888

| | | | | | | | | |
|---|---|---|---|---|---|---|---|---|
| St Giles in the Fields | 4457 | 3216 | St Katherines Tower | 956 | 601 | St Magdalens Bermond | 1943 | 1362 | St Mary Whitechap. | 4766 | 3855 |
| Hackney Parish | 232 | 132 | Lambeth Parish | 798 | 537 | St Mary Newington | 1272 | 1004 | Redriffe Parish | 304 | 210 |
| St James Clarkenwell | 1803 | 1377 | St Leonards Shoreditch | 2669 | 1949 | St Mary Islington | 696 | 593 | Stepney Parish | 8598 | 6583 |

Buried in the 12 out-Parishes in Middlesex and Surrey 28554    Whereof of the Plague 21420

| | | | | |
|---|---|---|---|---|
| St Clement Danes | 1969 | 1319 | St Mary Sauoy | 303 | 198 |
| St Paul Covent Garden | 408 | 261 | St Margaret Westm. | 4710 | 3742 |
| St Martins the Fields | 4804 | 2883 | *whereof at the Pesthouse* | 156 | |

*Buried in the 5 Parishes in the City and Liberties of Westminster.* 12194    *Whereof, of the Plague* — 8403

The Total of all the Christnings. — 9967
The Total of all the Burials this year — 97306
Whereof, of the Plague — 68596

## Diseases and Casualties this year.

| | | | | | |
|---|---|---|---|---|---|
| Abortive and Stillborne | 617 | Executed | 21 | Palfie | 30 |
| Aged | 1545 | Flox and Smal Pox | 655 | Plague | 68596 |
| Ague and Feaver | 5257 | Found dead in streets, fields, &c. | 20 | Plannet | 6 |
| Appoplex and Suddenly | 116 | French Pox | 86 | Plurisie | 15 |
| Bedrid | 10 | Frighted | 23 | Poysoned | 1 |
| Blasted | 5 | Gout and Sciatica | 27 | Quinsie | 35 |
| Bleeding | 16 | Grief | 46 | Rickets | 557 |
| Bloudy Flux, Scowring & Flux | 185 | Griping in the Guts | 1288 | Rifing of the Lights | 397 |
| Burnt and Scalded | 8 | Hang'd & made away themselves | 7 | Rupture | 34 |
| Calenture | 3 | Headmouldshot & Mouldfallen | 14 | Scurvy | 105 |
| Cancer, Gangrene and Fistula | 56 | Jaundies | 110 | Shingles and Swine pox | 2 |
| Canker, and Thrush | 111 | Impostume | 227 | Sores, Ulcers, broken and bruised | |
| Childbed | 625 | Kil'd by several accidents | 46 | Limbes | 82 |
| Chrisomes and Infants | 1258 | Kings Evill | 86 | Spleen | 14 |
| Cold and Cough | 68 | Leprosie | 2 | Spotted Feaver and Purples | 1929 |
| Collick and Winde | 134 | Lethargy | 14 | Stopping of the Stomach | 332 |
| Consumption and Tiffick | 4808 | Livergrowne | 20 | Stone and Strangury | 98 |
| Convulsion and Mother | 2036 | Meagrom and Headach | 12 | Surfet | 1251 |
| Distracted | 5 | Measles | 7 | Teeth and Worms | 2614 |
| Dropsie and Timpany | 1478 | Murthered, and Shot | 9 | Vomiting | 51 |
| Drowned | 50 | Overlaid and Starved | 45 | Vvenn | 1 |

Christned { Males — 5114, Females — 4853, In all — 9967 }
Buried { Males — 48569, Females — 48737, In all — 97306 } Of the Plague — 68596

Increased in the Burials in the 130 Parishes and at the Pest-house this year — 79009
Increased of the Plague in the 130 Parishes and at the Pest-house this year — 68590

in 1452, and these survive in continuous form from 1503. Similar runs of statistical information survive from Mantua (1496), Venice (1504) and Modena (1554). While records might be kept in a city beset by plague, the keeping of details year on year made the identification of a potential outbreak based on the recognition of a statistical pattern a possibility. This served as a way for magistrates to identify possible outbreaks, even if the people (and the clergy and medical practitioners) might be slow to notify the health officials.

Outside of Italy, France was fairly quick to implement many of these regulations. This is all the more impressive when one remembers that these bureaucratic structures were being introduced in a period during which religious strife was rending the state from end to end. The result of the national civil wars of religion was that individual cities (in which the republican tradition of local elected magistrates was very strong) rather than the national (royal) government implemented most plague regulations in France. Hence, plague ordinances were introduced at Troyes (1517), Reims (1522), and Paris (1531). By 1580, Paris had a permanent public health officer. The cost of these regulations was still the major problem impeding their adoption. Montpellier, in 1530, spent almost its entire annual revenue on plague expenditures. During outbreaks in the 1550s and 1575, Lille was forced to introduce special 'plague rates' to ensure the supply of sustenance to those confined at home or at the plague hospital. The best example of the lag between the acceptance of a 'good idea' from Italy and its implementation comes from Paris. In 1496, the French capital accepted that a plague hospital was essential, but ground was not broken for it until 1580. This abortive and incomplete structure was demolished soon thereafter. No structure was successfully completed until the construction of the Hôpital St Louis (constructed 1607-12), a full 116 years after the decision was taken to construct a purpose-built plague hospital.

Similar delays in implementation existed in the Low Countries. Again, the fact that the area was engaged in a war of revolt against the King of Spain and a religious reformation may well explain the delay. However, the strong local city councils allowed for regulations to be implemented in individual cities. In the 1590s, Amsterdam created a system to remove rubbish and added a plague doctor to the magisterial health committee. The plague hospital was built around a central courtyard. The entire structure was surrounded by canals and was located outside the city's walls. A further canal ran through the middle of the pest house, supplying the afflicted with drinking water. Zwolle set up a 'plague advisory body' along with a plague hospital in 1655. Good policy, in the Netherlands as well as elsewhere, was not necessarily synonymous with good practice. The pragmatic realities of money and bureaucratic sophistication or traditions in addition to major crises (for example, civil or religious strife) could delay or prevent the implementation of plague regulations, locally or nationally.

The grandeur of these regulations is best exemplified by the Milanese plague hospital. In 1488, the Lazaretto di San Gregorio was constructed. The plan was based on a monastic cloister with a central courtyard surrounded by ranges divided into individual rooms (cells). Although based on a monastic model, the building was enormous in scale. The courtyard measured 377.5 metres (413 yards) by 370 metres (403 yards). The surrounding building was divided into 288 separate rooms. The massive courtyard was able to accommodate plague victims in temporary tents or huts during the height of an outbreak and, in 1630, some 16,000 patients were housed in Milan's plague hospital. Clearly, this was a tremendously grand complex and would have cost an enormous amount of money to build and maintain. However, it stood the test of time. This late fifteenth-century structure was still able to awe and impress in 1646 – a century and a half after its construction – when John Evelyn (1620-1706) described it as a 'Cloyster, of a vast compasse: in earnest a royal fabric'.

In the mid-seventeenth century, Genoa boasted an equally impressive structure and system of plague quarantine. During a

*Two contemporary illustrations depicting famine (above) and plague (below) in Leiden in 1574. Note in the centre of the lower picture the child's coffin being carried aloft and the physician examining a specimen bottle.*

dispute with Florence, in which both cities quarantined and block-aded one another, a Florentine delegation was invited to Genoa to inspect the city's health in an effort to resolve the crisis. The mission from Florence was first taken to the pest house that lay outside the city's walls. The entrance, much to the delight of the Florentines, was guarded not by local troops who might be bribed but by trained professional German mercenaries. Inside, they were shown two separate quarantine areas. In the first, the *quarantina brutti*, there were fifty-five plague victims serving out (assuming they lived) a forty-day confinement followed by an additional period of convalescence. In the *spurga di sospetto*, 238 people were confined because they had had contact with plague victims or had arrived from areas where the disease was present. In the city's main hospital (Spedale Maggiore), the mission was shown 416 patients divided by gender and then treated according to four categories of illness: those suffering from a fever, those needing surgical inter-vention, children with fevers, and convalescents. Finally, the Florentines were taken to the hospice for the incurably ill (Spedale degli Incurabili), which housed 698 inmates, including syphlitics and the insane. From a population of 80,000, the Florentine dele-gation saw 1,114 people (1.4 per cent of the population) being treated in the various hospitals. They concluded that the city was in good health.

As a result of the impressive arrangements for public health found in both Genoa and Florence, the Genoese suggested, in the same year, that their two states join with Naples and Rome in organising an international system of plague quarantine and block-ade. They wanted each state to standardise their rules to a single norm and to agree that any area interdicted (as plague infected) would immediately be blocked by the other three. This short-lived attempt at extra-national plague regulations collapsed by 1656 without ever gaining the full participation of Rome and Naples. Nevertheless, it highlights the awareness of smaller city-states that an effective, preventative quarantine and blockade had to be organised on a large geographical basis. Once plague was at a city's gates, there was little that even the best ordinances and most vigilant health committees could do.

❖　　　❖　　　❖

The cost and complexity of plague regulations was not the only difficulty facing city councils and national governments trying to mitigate against the worst ravages of the disease. Plague was, in itself, 'treacherous'. That is, it was extremely hard to identify the first appearance of pestilence. Many localities were only aware that an outbreak was imminent when they were already in the midst of it. Most medical practitioners were able, in theory, to give an accurate and detailed list of the symptoms recognisable in a normal case of plague. The Florentine doctor Antonio Pellicini, in 1630, stated that plague victims presented with 'severe headache, anxious insomnia, mental derangement, burning thirst, lack of appetite, panting respiration, continuous anxiety, bitter vomiting, foul diarrhoea, cloudy urine, very infelicitous pulse, burning face and eyes, dry and black tongue, unusual facial expression, and unspeakable prostration'.

However, many of these symptoms were present in other diseases and some plague cases would have few, if any, of the above. For example, cases of pneumonic and septicaemic plague, while rare, killed so quickly that few symptoms had time to develop. More importantly, the incubation period of the disease meant that it was often identifiable only in its later stages. The only sure and universally accepted proof of plague was the appearance of the buboes and accompanying skin blotches caused by subcutaneous haemorrhaging. As Rondinelli said in Florence in 1631: 'physicians were frequently summoned by the Health Magistracy [professional politicians not medical men] … some physicians maintained that it was a plague, others denied it, and not for the pleasure of contradiction but because they believe it so'.

In addition to the basic difficulties of identifying a bacterial infection solely on the basis of external symptoms, there was the added problem that most states did not want to be informed that plague was actually present. In 1630, in the town of Busto Arsizio, the doctor who gave official confirmation that an epidemic was present was shot dead. Moreover, common people often conspired to hide the presence of plague. The Venetian authorities, studying their death statistics, noted an abnormally large number of deaths on the island of Malamocco. Suspecting plague, they exhumed three recently buried corpses and subjected them to a post-mortem. Buboes were found and the island was immediately quarantined. In addition to exhumation, a more general programme of post-mortems and autopsies was frequently used. However, since most medical practitioners were unable to differentiate between alterations to a body caused by disease and those caused by decay, the process was of little value (and tended to offend relatives).

In the end, even Italy had to accept that all of their plague regulations, bureaucracies, hospitals and other efforts had failed to limit the virulence of the disease. When plague appeared (albeit less frequently), one could – and should – expect that one quarter to one half of the population would die. Death in individuals – whether at home, on the street or in the pest house – would occur within days of the first appearance of any symptoms, the first usually being a high fever. Physicians and magistrates did notice patterns to the mortality. For example, in the Genoa of 1656, Father Antero Maria da San Bonaventura observed that 'the privilege of the rich consists of their being able to avoid the plague while the privilege of the poor consists of the fact that they can survive the plague [being naturally hardier than the pampered and effete rich] when they catch it'. Nevertheless, four centuries of observation failed to produce any remedy. It is hardly surprising, therefore, that one English minister, perhaps ironically, was led to prescribe 'a quart of the repentance of Ninevah and put thereto both your handfuls of fervent [faith] in Christ's blood, with as much hope and charity of the purest you can get in God's shop'. Or, as another more succinctly said: 'cease vexing heaven, and cease to die'.

❖        ❖        ❖

It is perhaps worth departing for a moment from the vexed and problematic world of the magistrate to consider the impact of plague on individuals. What did the common people do when plague was declared? Clearly, for the reasons already recounted, they did everything they could to avoid and circumvent the attempts of the State to control them under the guise of controlling the epidemic. Physicians were of little help since they still felt, as Giovan Agostino Contardo of Genoa put it, that 'prevention is much more noble and more necessary than therapy'. In addition, they tended to flee at the first hint of plague. Those who did remain were unlikely to be of much help. Throughout the history of plague, the comments of physicians evidence a complete inability to rise above their theoretical presuppositions. For example, the pathetic irony of Father Antero's comment on his special plague outfit, in 1657, is palpable; they were 'good only to protect one from fleas which cannot nest in it'. He complained of the fleas but considered them only as a nuisance: 'I have to change my clothes frequently if I do not want to be devoured by the fleas ... I can swear to you that none of the bodily torments which one must endure in the *lazaretto* can compare to the fleas'.

It was the condition in the pest houses that frightened most common people even more than the possibility of house quarantine. As Cardinal Spada noted, after inspecting a plague hospital: 'you are overwhelmed by intolerable smells ... you cannot walk but among corpses ... This is an exact reproduction of hell'. It is hardly surprising that there was a tremendous market for self-help works on plague prevention and cure. Most people hoped, as did their rulers, to avoid the plague or to lessen its impact. Concoctions ranged from special drinks to poultices to variants on aromatherapy. The basic ingredients of all these remedies were any or all of the following: rue, rosemary, onions, vinegar, wormwood and various opiate derivatives. Chemical physicians (though despised and ridiculed by traditional, philosophically-trained physicians) also recommended various amulets containing arsenic, as well as the use of tin and mercury. This poison was meant to 'draw out' the plague's venom on the principle that 'like attracts like'. For similar reasons, people made use of compounds derived from vipers, scorpions and poisonous toads. Other popular remedies called for the use of filed horses' hooves, coral, crabs' eyes and claws. One poultice recipe – to be applied directly to the buboes – combined honey, duck fat, turpentine, soot, treacle, egg yolks and scorpion oil.

The common people also had ways of dealing with the state's rules on burials. In every case, people strongly resented and resisted attempts to bury their loved ones in pits rather than sacred ground around the local parish church. The use of mass graves served two purposes for the State. First, the pragmatic excuse was simple expediency – the large number of bodies had to be disposed of quickly. Second, the decay of plague bodies might produce infected (miasmic) gasses that could rise out of the ground and cause further infections. Thus, burials outside of the town and the extensive use of lime to dissolve the bodies was a medical necessity. However, despite the threats of infection, common people made it clear that they were opposed to the anonymity and barbarity of these mass burials. They did not want their relatives and neighbours layered into a pit 'like lasagne', as one Italian chronicler put it. Thus, in 1603, a London observer noted that 'the poorer sort, yea women with young children, will flock to burials, and stand over open [mass] graves … that all the world may see that they fear not the Plague'. In 1710, the population of the small Swedish settlement of Blekinge exhumed the bodies of a plague pit and reburied the corpses in the local parish cemetery. It would seem that neither fear of contagion nor of miasma was capable of wholly severing the bonds of love and friendship amongst the poorest in society, despite the frequent mention in literate sources of heartlessness among the socially better-off.

Resistance by individuals in society to the introduction of these new regulations and State intrusion was evident at every level in fact. Gravediggers resented being told that they would not be allowed to keep the best set of clothes of a deceased, although this was their traditional wage. Governments wanted these clothes destroyed instead of being sold to the second-hand clothing merchants by the gravediggers. Wealthier merchants, who often depended on the free movement of trade goods (especially cloth) were more than able to prevent the implementation of plague regulations, as they did in Venice in 1629. The delay in establishing an effective *cordon sanitaire* allowed the plague to enter the city. Women often took direct action by burning pest houses, as they did in Salisbury (1627) and Colchester (1631). In Florence, women quarantined in the plague house chanted from the windows until they were able to incite a local mob of youths to riot for their release; the local health magistrate resigned in fear of his life.

Some states recognised the fervour of popular resistance and attempted to ameliorate the severity of the regulations. In the Dutch Republic, people were actively encouraged to visit plague victims on their deathbeds. The quarantined were allowed to take walks 'for the air', as long as they carried white sticks signifying their infectious state. Moreover, the people quarantined with a plague victim at home were advised to attend church services as long as they remained uninfected. It is impossible adequately to explain the Dutch attitude, but it may well be a feature of the Calvinism adopted in the Republic. Many observers commented that those who held to a stronger view of predestination tended to be less concerned about possible infection. In theory, a belief in predestination should have produced an attitude similar to that held in the Islamic world. Ministers of a Calvinistic bent in England seem to have been of such a mind:

> The Puritans say that [plague] should not be avoided, that it is [a bless-
> ing] to die of plague, and that although they are close to [the disease], it
> will not attack any but those already singled out by God, [no matter
> what they do]. That this is infallible and that it is a false madness to try
> to guard against it.

The Spanish Catholic visitor who noted this Puritan theory was,
perhaps with a sense of malicious humour, led to comment on
their practice by adding that for 'all that, I think a great many of
them leave London [during an outbreak]'.

Thus, plague was not the only thing endemic (or native) to
European society during the last two centuries of the Second
Pandemic. The various governments settled on a specific bureaucratic approach to controlling the chaos attendant upon a
plague outbreak. Once this methodology was developed, almost no
alterations were made. Indeed, countries continued to adopt these
rules and regulations over a century after their development, when
every bit of evidence suggested that they did not work
and, as in the case of home quarantine, probably made the situation
worse. Finally, just as plague and plague regulations were a part
of the cyclical rhythm of life in Western Europe for nearly three
centuries, popular resistance to state control was a recurring
reality. Not only did experience teach people that neither the
physicians nor the magistrates had any idea of how to prevent, contain or cure plague, but also that the rules and regulations
were counter-productive. Many aspects of the Italian model were
seen as dangerous during plague outbreaks and dangerously
intrusive the rest of the time. People objected to outsiders examining the corpses of their dead relatives and they fiercely resisted
autopsies. They disliked the ability of the State to exhume
bodies without their consent or to dump their loved ones in pits
heaving with decaying corpses and lime. Intrusions into their livelihoods and business practices were resented. The closing of markets
and the interruption of trade were likely to destroy even those that

had survived the epidemic. For example, in 1630, the normal number of Florentines on state benefit was 12,000 from a population of 80,000. During the outbreak of that year, this number soared to 30,000, implying that an extra 18,000 poor people were not able or allowed to earn a living wage. Those few who were still making a living were forced to meet the extra tax burden necessary to support the 1,070 plague workers, 23 mules and 186 carts required to care for the sick, the quarantined and the unemployed.

❖     ❖     ❖

A brief study of plague in Pistoia in 1630-31 gives a clear idea of the impact of plague on a city thoroughly equipped with the best regulatory system then available. The city had a *lazaretto* but 'most of the beds are without sheets and few have blankets ... the patients are five to a bed, to the detriment of [those recovering] who, because of close contact with [the] contagion, suffer relapses'. Despite the conditions, the pest house managed to care for 1,198 patients in an eleven-month period (October 1630–August 1631) of whom 607 died (51 per cent). Many, however, were quarantined at home and, considering the rapid course of the disease, died there before they could be moved to the pest house. Of the 125 house confinements, eleven were in homes belonging to the wealthy ruling elite, fifteen were artisans who had sufficient cash reserves to care for themselves and a further ninety-nine were poor artisans who were forced to rely on the State help to feed themselves behind their locked doors.

In a normal year, city revenues brought in 28,000 scudi (roughly 2,300 per month). This plague outbreak cost at least 9,100 scudi (830 per month) or the equivalent of 36 per cent of the state's normal income. How could a small town afford such excessive demands on the public purse, especially in a crisis that, by its very nature, meant the collapse of the tax base? The records of the health committee show that only 3 per cent of the money spent on the plague actually came from normal revenue sources. Since the normal annual expenditures still had to be met and the revenues fell dramatically during a plague outbreak, 52 per cent of the health committee's budget came from loans. Finally, a surprising 45 per cent of the money disbursed during the plague came from charitable sources.

The role of charity in dealing with plague is extremely important. Although the Western European states were more than willing to regulate the lives of their poorer citizens, they were rarely able to force their wealthier citizens to pay to cover the cost of an outbreak. Thus, charity remained an important part of the financial equation. States were not forced to tax because the charitable sector of the economy was large, wealthy and, to a surprising degree, controlled by the same magistrates (sitting as trustees) who decided not to tax themselves or their fellows. Thus, in Pistoia, three charitable trusts, which had originally been set up by wealthy benefactors to provide for the common good (and whose assets were regularly augmented by subsequent bequests), were the main sources of additional funds. Of the 3,575 scudi from trusts, 1,244 (35 per cent) came from these three. Another 500 scudi were gifted to the city by the *Monte di Pietà* bank, which was a publicly-owned bank designed to aid poorer artisans. The bank was obliged by its charter to give its profits to the public good. Another 400 scudi came from alms collected in plague relief boxes set up in the churches, and a further 100 came from other sources. In all, the health committee received 10,110 scudi to pay for the implementation of the plague regulations, only about 300 of which came from normal governmental revenues and taxes. In addition, one trust gave wheat worth another 2,320 scudi. This represented a total additional income for plague expenses equivalent to 1.25 scudi per person (from a population of 8,000) in a city which normally collected 3.5 scudi per person.

The health committee was then in a position to dispense, at its discretion, an enormous sum of money. It is hardly surprising that many magistracies were loath to create permanent health boards with extensive powers and enormous budgets. The Pistoia committee spent a total of 9,170 scudi before the plague ended (thus showing a small profit of 940 scudi, or 9 per cent, of their overall budget). Of this figure, a full 53 per cent was spent on food. This was necessary to ensure that the patients in the pest house and those people confined at home would not starve. The next largest expenditure was on wages for the hospital workers, which accounted for 24 per cent of the funds. In all, the committee employed about sixty workers (one worker per 130 citizens). 10 per cent of the budget went towards the maintenance of the committee's buildings (primarily the pest house), and the final 13 per cent of the money was spent on a number of minor expenditures.

This close examination of a plague outbreak at the very end of the period under consideration highlights a number of features of the decades after the development of the Italian regulations in the fifteenth century. First, even an extremely well-organised town like Pistoia was unable to employ its rules to prevent, contain or stop the plague. Second, the enthusiasm of the State for these regulatory methods is evident in its willingness to expend enormous sums of money on a system that had never shown success. Third, the level of reliance on charitable giving implies that societies were making extensive provisions through these trusts for periods of crisis. In effect, the magisterially-controlled private trusts served as a social security insurance system. Fourth, even in a very 'mild' outbreak of plague (less than 12 per cent of the population of Pistoia died), the society was subjected to enormous burdens and stresses. Finally, the ability of the state to enforce these regulations during a serious and costly crisis gives some idea of how successful the government (its leaders and officials) had been at imposing a system of bureaucratic order on its populace. The appeal of such a system to a society's rulers is immediately apparent.

An even better example of the role of plague regulations in state formation and social control can be found in a survey of their introduction into England. Although England was probably the most centralised and bureaucratic state in early modern Europe, it was surprisingly slow in adopting the Italian model. Indeed, it might be argued that the sophistication of English bureaucracy was one reason why the ordinances were difficult to implement. In most states, these regulations were used as a means of strengthening the power and oversight of the government with regard to its citizenry. However, in England, the state was already sufficiently strong so as not to need this methodology of social control. Moreover, a highly developed and powerful bureaucracy is likely to be very resistant to the introduction of alternative power bases (such as health boards). This proved to be the case in England, where well-organised and well-established bureaucracies (for example, the Corporation of the City of London) were loath to derogate some of their traditional powers to new bodies. They were even less enthusiastic about innovations that introduced completely new bodies and (financial) responsibilities into their already complex political and economic structures.

The fact that England was slow to adopt Italian-style regulations should not be taken to mean that the English were uninterested in the best means of controlling plague or medical developments elsewhere. Indeed, in the period 1486-1604, over 150 books, treatises and pamphlets about medicine were printed in England and nearly two dozen of these dealt specifically with plague. In 1625-27 alone, thirty-six books on plague were published. Many of these works drew heavily on Continental sources and evidence a keen interest amongst the literate English public for up-to-date information on medicine and plague. Nevertheless, it is clear that the various levels of the Tudor (and later Stuart) state were slow to adopt and implement the generally accepted regime of plague rules – this despite the seventeen general crises of mortality between 1500 and 1670. In addition, north of the border, Scottish towns were making efforts to control the entry of infected people and goods, to quarantine the infected, and to segregate those in contact with the infected by the late 1400s. Since the central government in Scotland was relatively weak, the towns and cities took the lead in implementing plague regulations in much the same manner as French urban areas were doing in the same period.

The first attempt to regulate the nation during times of plague in England demonstrates the greater stress placed upon bureaucratic development rather than plague prevention. There was a nationwide outbreak of plague in 1498 and again in 1535, but it was in 1518 that the first attempt was made to introduce some set of ordinances for the nation. Again, the second major period of activity by the state was to come in 1578. The previous major pestilential attack had been in 1563 and plague was not to return until 1589. Thus, unlike most Continental areas, the proclamation of plague ordinances in England was not directly related to a major outbreak of the disease. In a sense, one might argue that in England the attempts to regulate society in times of plague was less a knee-jerk reaction to an epidemic crisis and more a response to considered thought on the subject.

Prior to 1518, most foreigners travelling in England noted the almost total lack of preparedness for a plague attack. However, in that year, Cardinal Wolsey (*c.*1475-1530) attempted to introduce a range of bureaucratic reforms designed to make the state more efficient and to prepare it for periods of crisis. Plague regulations, therefore, were part of a general attempt at governmental reform and rationalisation. On 13 January 1518, regulations were proclaimed ordering that any infected house was to be marked by a bundle of straw and quarantined for forty days. Any uninfected person confined in these houses was able to go outside, but had to carry a white stick to signify their possible contamination. In April, Sir Thomas More (1478-1535) introduced these rules in Oxford. The involvement of Wolsey and More highlights the fact that this was simply part of the general attempt at that time (supported by the King) to introduce Continental aspects of Renaissance monarchy. The state was not simply trying to bring medical and health regulations in line with the most advanced practices of the Continent. Rather, there was a general attempt to reform the entire structure of the state and society in keeping with patterns already articulated on the Continent. A similar process was being undertaken by the French Crown and its officials under Francis I (1494-1547).

In addition to the rules on house confinement, the reforms of this period involved a whole range of non-medical ordinances. In 1517, Wolsey undertook a general enquiry on the progress of enclosure (agricultural and land-ownership reform) and sumptuary legislation was introduced (to control social and cultural mobility). Moreover, there was a campaign against vagrancy and begging in London; this was certainly related to concepts of sanitation, health and pollution, as well as social control. Finally, the single most important development with relation to health was the founding, in 1518, of the Royal College of Physicians in London. However, the more general range of plague regulations was slow to be adopted and, in many cases, individual cities and towns were making the best advances on their own initiative. For example, in 1537-45, most provincial towns moved to isolate plague victims in pest houses (recommended as the best possible action), while London, with many more people (and, thus, victims), was forced to rely almost wholly on home quarantine. In 1550-70, most of the country had accepted the governmental directives that the infected and those in contact with them had to be isolated, but there remained considerable resistance to any moves to introduce mechanisms for paying for the quarantine. By 1574-85, however, most cities had ambitious regulations (theoretically) in place. Indeed, so seemingly successful was the process that, in 1580, a royal proclamation declared that the health of the nation was 'in better estate universally than hath been in man's memory'.

The reality was that the implementation of plague regulations was still very haphazard and not uniform across the country. In 1578, the Crown undertook an official review of the situation in England. Many of the problems uncovered were those that had been identified in a report submitted to William Cecil (1520-98), Lord Burghley, in 1563 by Cesare Adelmare, a Paduan-educated physician. He said that there was still no effective health and welfare bureaucracy in the localities, let alone the nation. Also, what system there was lacked a secure financial basis from which effectively to operate. In conclusion, he strongly recommended that England, both at the national level and in individual towns and cities, should adopt the entire system and structure of plague regulations as they were being practised in Italy. In 1578, the Privy Council made a concerted attempt to move the Elizabethan state in that direction.

At the request of the Privy Council, the Royal College of Physicians drew up a list of medical actions that should be under-taken in any plague outbreak. They recommended that perfumes and fumigants should be used to cleanse the air, infected goods and structures. Clothing and bedding should be changed frequently and used cloth should be washed or, better, burned. Finally, they advised the use of traditional curatives (for example, rue and wormwood). The Privy Council then produced a set of guidelines for Justices of the Peace. These were very comprehensive, though they did not gain the force of law until 1604.

The Privy Council directed Justices to meet every three weeks during an epidemic to review the situation. They were to receive regular reports from seekers and watchers (those set to identify victims and to ensure that quarantines were not broken). The Justices were to implement a regular tax that would ensure that sufficient money was on hand to deal with a plague outbreak. In effect, the state was attempting to introduce a permanent 'plague rate'. The clothing and bedding of victims was to be burned. All funerals should be held at dusk to minimise the number of people attending. The Privy Council also insisted that home quarantine should be observed very strictly and should last a full six weeks. Watchmen were to be employed to ensure the confinement was not broken. By 1620-25, the state was able to convince most local-ities of the need to isolate the infected and, more importantly, to pay for the cost of the quarantines at home or in the pest houses.

The one great exception to the process was the situation in London. By 1583, the Privy Council and Corporation had reached a broad agreement on regulations but there remained a serious disagreement about quarantine. The City preferred home confinement to pest houses, arguing that it simply could not afford to maintain sufficient beds, buildings and workers for the task. They supported their position by pointing out that they did not have authority over the whole of suburban London, though they would be expected to cope with plague victims from the entire area during an outbreak. Also, they argued that liberties and charters given to the Royal College and the Bishop of London meant that in many areas they were not empowered to command, even in the city. On one level, the Corporation and Council were clashing over the questions of bureaucracy and jurisdiction. In the ordered and well-developed English system, traditional boundaries were hard to

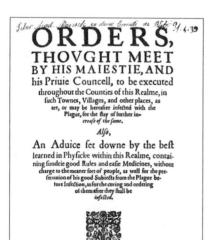

*Measures published by the Privy Council in England in 1625 intended to prevent infection by plague and the spread of the disease. It was published with advice from medical experts on possible remedies and cures for the disease.*

overcome. In effect, the strength of English officials and agencies made it difficult, if not impossible, to introduce wholesale, foreign rationalisation. Just as importantly, the Corporation argued that any confinement was not a good idea, stating in 1583 that 'to shut up the sound and infected together seemeth by experience rather to increase than decrease the infection'. The leaders of the City had correctly identified one of the most obvious weaknesses of the Italian system: clearly, it did not decrease the mortality rate, and some on the Continent were beginning to reason that aspects of the system (especially the confinement of the uninfected) was positively detrimental. In a compromise solution, the Privy Council recommended, in 1609, that those who were actually infected should be confined to separate rooms inside a sealed house.

Under Charles I (1600-49), a more concerted effort was made to convert London into a capital fit for a seventeenth-century monarch. He and his advisors wanted to extend royal authority along the lines of governmental and absolutist theories being developed on the Continent. In 1630, the Royal College recommended the end of home quarantine and the construction of enough pest houses to meet the capital's needs in an epidemic. They highlighted that this was the practice already adopted in the great cities of Europe (and advanced Paris, Venice and Padua as examples). They specifically pointed to the Hôpital St Louis of Henry IV (1553-1610) as an ideal.

In 1631, the King received a report prepared by Sir Theodore de Mayerne, a Huguenot physician. He identified a number of problems in London: poverty, drunkenness, homelessness, public begging, overcrowded homes, and unregulated building construction. He advised that a permanent, salaried corps of physicians, surgeons and apothecaries should be appointed to oversee the health and sanitation of London. Further, he explicitly condemned home quarantine. He suggested that London needed four or five large pest houses. The pest houses should be used to care for and confine those actually infected with the disease. Anyone who had had contact with a plague victim should be quarantined separately for forty days; he suggested that these people might reasonably be confined at home. He identified, in addition to the normal cats and dogs, that vermin (rats, mice, weasels and such) were a threat to public health. Finally, he recommended strongly that a temporary body of magistrates (a health board) should be appointed with absolute executive power to oversee the implementation of necessary regulations during an outbreak. The Privy Council reacted to the report by noting that these rules were 'used in other countries and found to be the safer course'. Another Huguenot, Louis du Moulin, writing in 1641, strongly supported Mayerne's conclusions.

The intervention of the Civil War and the collapse of the royalist state meant that the innovations and reforms recommended by Mayerne and Moulin were not implemented. The period of the Commonwealth saw only one major alteration to the traditional rules (that is, the ordinances and laws from 1578-1609). At long last, the government did impose full national blockades and quarantines on any goods, people or ships coming from areas suspected of having plague. This meant that ships were regularly quarantined with their cargoes and personnel at some point distant from the docks until the officials in the given port were convinced that there was no disease on board.

The late adoption of Italian regulations was not, as we have seen, a function of English isolation or anti-Continental sentiment. Virtually everyone accepted that the measures developed and implemented on the Continent were the most effective means of preventing or ameliorating the impact of a plague. However, in most places on the Continent (and in Scotland), the regulations were an impetus for the development of strong, centralised bureaucracies of state. England already had an extremely well-developed system of local, national and royal government. In the circumstances of the English state, the plague regulations and health boards were not so much an innovative step in the development of bureaucracies as a tremendous alteration to, and reform of, pre-existent bodies. These groups were very jealous of their traditional powers, and had the position and strength to resist attempts to rationalise them into a foreign model. England, more than most political societies, identified and resisted the social control and order aspects of the regulations at an official level. For the rest of Europe, the moves to introduce strong bureaucracies were embraced by officials as a way of augmenting their power and position. In England, politicians and officials feared the plague regulations as intrusions into their spheres. Common people across Europe resisted the introduction and extension of 'order'; the English common people found allies in local officials who, from their point of view, were fearful of a 'new order'.

# Five

# DEATH'S FINALE
## The Great London Plague
## 1665

*Everybody is talking of this dead, and that man sick, and so many in this place
and so many in that.*

Samuel Pepys

hroughout the previous chapters, there have been a number of recurring themes. The introduction and adoption of
Italian style responses to, and regulations for, plague is one of the most
striking. Likewise, the constant attempt by individuals at every level
of society to undermine these ordinances is apparent. Within every
society and culture, there existed a remarkable tension. Everyone
wanted to prevent any appearance of plague or to contain and eliminate the pestilence once it attacked. However, on an individul basis,
people wanted to avoid the costly impact on their own lives of the
plague regulations. No one wanted to be confined at home with a
dead or dying relative. Hence, many tried to conceal suspicious
deaths and diseases. People did not want their goods destroyed, so
they lied yet again. Going to the pest house was clearly a death
sentence, so everyone strove to avoid being seen as infected. At every
stage, the fear and greed of individual people worked to undermine
the best-laid plans of health committees and city councils.

However, even at the level of leadership and government, the same fear and greed could work to undermine the ordinances designed to protect the citizenry from disease. Most councils were keen to avoid declaring the presence of plague since they feared the detrimental impact on trade that a quarantine or blockade would bring. Leaders sought to delay popular panic by hiding the first cases of plague or by downplaying its impact through false statistics. Medical advice was ignored or rejected outright if it was felt that its implementation would too greatly undermine society, cultural norms or the economy. Time and time again, practical, pragmatic issues of politics and business led civic leaders to hesitate and pre-varicate in dealing with an outbreak. All of these responses, both personal and official, were evident in the London plague of 1665. Indeed, it is perhaps possible to ask whether this vacillation in the face of a serious health crisis is simply a feature of plague or a wider expression of something inherent in human psyches and cultures.

❖     ❖     ❖

At the end of April, the government announced that forty-two people had been struck down by a virulent, highly contagious pestilential epidemic. The disease had not been seen in the capital for nearly a decade, and medical experts were unable to suggest any adequate cure or preventative for the plague. Responding to this uncertainty, the various state bodies were forced to re-issue those measures that had been taken in the previous outbreaks over the last century. Those who were infected, or who had been in contact with the infected, were either to withdraw to one of the city's hospitals or to lock themselves in their homes. Those who remained confined in their houses were promised that the city would provide workers and medical personnel to visit them and to ensure that they were supplied with the necessaries for life. However, the Privy Council and the Corporation assured people that there would be no need to raise local taxes since the extra expens-es would be met out of current receipts and from various charitable and private donations from across the country. Although many doubted that the sums would be sufficient, the population remained relatively calm while they waited to see if these deaths were isolated cases or harbingers of a more general epidemic.

By the end of May, with 700 deaths, many began to suspect that the disease was becoming more widespread. For the most part, though, the infection seemed confined to the poorer parts of the metropolis. Since the best medical advice held that the disease was more likely to strike the socially deprived, the city moved to limit the movement of people within London in an attempt to contain the pestilence to the poorer and more densely-populated parts of the city. The Privy Council also ordered landlords to clear those on shorter leases or in smaller, crowded accommodation from their homes in an effort to alleviate the overcrowded conditions that were thought to encourage plague. Some of the wealthier residents of the city were also reported to have begun to evacuate their spouses and children, either to their summer places or to relatives living in other parts of England. Although there were minor disruptions, for the most part, the city went about its normal business.

Throughout the month of June, the situation steadily worsened. On 5 June, the mayor closed all places of public entertainment, such as theatres. By the middle of the month, many people had fled the city – including the monarch. The courts were closed and most barristers left the capital. Despite the publication of numerous self-help manuals (forty-six were published in the course of the year) relating to the epidemic, the death toll continued to rise. In the first week of June, a further 700 deaths were reported to the authorities and announced publicly on the printed *Bills of Mortality*. The next week, the total doubled to 1,400 with 2,800 dead in the third week. The June total was pushed higher with 4,200 deaths in the last week. The month's final total reached over 9,000 dead (over 300 per day). Moreover, the spread of the disease to neighbouring towns and cities forced Oxbridge and other educational establishments to announce their closure for the foreseeable future.

The plague continued to worsen in July. The mayor announced that all schools would close until the end of September at the earliest. Fearing the continuing spread of the pestilence, the monarch fled farther from London, finally settling in Oxford where the architecture of the older colleges made it possible tightly to regulate entry and exit. It was hoped that this would limit any possible infection. By October, the plague forced parliament to join the Crown in Oxford. For the moment, though, the situation in London was the primary concern. Announcements by health officials revealed that the death toll for July from all causes had reached 123,900, with 79,100 directly attributed to the disease.

While quarantine regulations in other neighbouring areas made it difficult to flee the city, persons of substance and wealth were still able to get away. However, their important business operations were such that some were forced periodically to come back into the city while some stayed throughout, determined to defend their properties and interests against collapse or lawlessness. Many leading figures in the city complained that too many officeholders and people in positions of responsibility were fleeing the city and their civic responsibilities. Even the Bishop of London was forced to warn clergy that those who fled would find themselves out of a job upon their return.

Opposite page:

Above left: *A proclamation from the Mayor of London in July 1665, imposing certain restrictions during the plague. These include closing public houses and schools, prohibiting singing or hawking goods in the street, dealing with vagrants and ensuring that the corpses of cats, dogs and other vermin are cleared from the streets.*

Above right: *A copy of the burial register at Cripplegate, London, recording the deaths that were the result of plague during August 1665.*

Below left: *A bill recording burials in London during one week of August 1665.*

Below right: *The reverse of the bill, with a breakdown of causes of death.*

## By the Mayor.

To the Alderman of the Ward of

As a farther meanes (by Gods blessing) then what is before directed to obviate the encrease of the Plague within this City and Liberties, we are to put and cause to be put in present and effectual execution, within your Ward, the several Orders following, besides and overpeach by our and our Successors, in the Court of Aldermen, in that behalf.

1. That no Vintner, Inholder, Cook, Ordinary-keeper, Seller of strong waters, Ale house-keeper, or Coffee-house keeper, shall henceforward, during this infection receive or entertain any person or persons into their houses or shops, (save onely the travelling Guests or Passengers) but soberly and in moderation; That that others who make these Accommodations may receive the same at due hours, or forth for, as they need.

2. That your Watchmen attend to enquire weekly of all Masters and Disorders committed in any Tavern, Inne, Ordinary, Ale-house, Coffee-house, or other place of common entertainment, contrary to the Order before mentioned, to otherwise against the Laws and Customes of this City, and that he of all other Offences within their inquiry, especially Disorders, and such like, as are most pernicious, and make due presentment thereof unto you, that thereupon present course may be taken for correction and punishing of the person offending contrary to Law.

3. That present and effectual course be taken to search within your wards of Inmates or Undertenants, which have been a principal means of increasing the Infection within this City and parts adjacent.

4. That none be suffered to sing or say Ballads in the Streets, or to sell, by way of Hawking, any Goods or Commodities whatsoever.

5. That all Grammar Schools, Writing Schools, and other Schools for the teaching of youth or Children of either sex, be suddenly and peremptorily dismissed, unless the Court of Aldermen shall otherwise make or restrain. And especially that Dancing-Schools, and Fencing Schools, and all meetings there, be utterly prohibited and peremptorily shut up, until the Court take other order.

6. That a careful Watch and Ward be constantly kept at the Gates and Landing places, to restrain and prevent the ingress of all Vagrants, Beggers, loose and dangerous people, from the out parts into this City and Liberties, and to bring to punishment such as shall be apprehended being of that kind, according to Law.

7. That Dogs, Cats and other Vermin, kill or lying dead in the Street be duly carried away (as the laws and order both) by the Raker of every Ward.

8. That the Churchwardens, Constables and other Officers, (whom it concerns) be very active and diligent in searching, before and punish all untouched and unorderly Tipling, Gaming, Labouring, Working upon the Lords of Towns, and other Offences whatsoever, to the uttermost punishment of the Laws. And to employ their utmost endeavours for the hue and cry upon infectious thereof. And, for better notice of these Orders, you are to find Copies thereof to the Ministers of the several Parishes within your Ward, who are desired to read the same in their Churches the next Lords day.

And thereof fail you not, as you mind the health and welfare of the City. Dated at the Guildhall, London, the fourth day of July, 1665.

Weld.

Printed by James Flesher, Printer to the Honourable City of LONDON.

---

---

## London 35    From the 15 of August to the 22. 1665

| | Bur. | Plag. | | Bur. | Plag. |
|---|---|---|---|---|---|
| S¹ Alban Woodstreet | 11 | 8 | S¹ George Botolphlane | — | 4 |
| Alhallows Barking | 15 | 11 | S¹ Gregory by S¹ Pauls | 9 | 6 |
| Alhallows Breadstreet | — | — | S¹ Hellens | 11 | 1 |
| Alhallows Great | 6 | 5 | S¹ James Dukes place | 7 | 5 |
| Alhallows Honylane | — | — | S¹ James Garlickhithe | 5 | 3 |
| Alhallows Lesse | 2 | 2 | S¹ John Baptist | 7 | 4 |
| Alhallows Lumbardstreet | 3 | 1 | S¹ John Evangelist | — | — |
| Alhallows Stayning | 7 | 5 | S¹ John Zachary | 3 | 2 |
| Alhallows the Wall | 18 | 11 | S¹ Katharine Coleman | 7 | 4 |
| S¹ Alphage | 18 | 10 | S¹ Katharine Creechurch | 17 | 7 |
| S¹ Andrew Hubbard | — | — | S¹ Lawrence Jewry | — | — |
| S¹ Andrew Undershaft | 14 | 9 | S¹ Lawrence Pountney | 4 | 2 |
| S¹ Andrew Wardrobe | 21 | 16 | S¹ Leonard Eastcheap | — | — |
| S¹ Ann Aldersgate | 18 | 11 | S¹ Leonard Fosterlane | 17 | 13 |
| S¹ Ann Blackfryars | 22 | 17 | S¹ Magnus Parish | 1 | 1 |
| S¹ Antholins Parish | — | — | S¹ Margaret Lothbury | — | — |
| S¹ Austins Parish | — | — | S¹ Margaret Moses | — | — |
| S¹ Bartholomew Exchange | 2 | 2 | S¹ Margaret Newfishstreet | 3 | 2 |
| S¹ Bennet Fynck | — | — | S¹ Margaret Pattons | — | — |
| S¹ Bennet Gracechurch | — | — | S¹ Mary Abchurch | 2 | 2 |
| S¹ Bennet Paulswharf | 16 | 8 | S¹ Mary Aldermanbury | 11 | 9 |
| S¹ Bennet Sherehog | — | — | S¹ Mary Aldermary | 2 | 1 |
| S¹ Botolph Billingsgate | 2 | 2 | S¹ Mary le Bow | — | — |
| Christs Church | 17 | 12 | S¹ Mary Bothaw | — | — |
| S¹ Christophers | — | — | S¹ Mary Colechurch | — | — |
| S¹ Clement Eastcheap | — | — | S¹ Mary Hill | 2 | 1 |
| S¹ Dionis Backchurch | — | — | S¹ Mary Mountaw | 2 | 2 |
| S¹ Dunstan East | 7 | 2 | S¹ Mary Sommerset | 5 | 3 |
| S¹ Edmund Lumbardst. | 2 | 1 | S¹ Mary Stayning | — | — |
| S¹ Edenborough | 17 | 7 | S¹ Mary Woolchurch | — | — |
| S¹ Faith | 6 | 6 | S¹ Mary Woolnoth | 4 | 1 |
| S¹ Foster | 13 | 11 | S¹ Martin Iremongerlane | — | — |
| S¹ Gabriel Fenchurch | — | — | | | |

| | Bur. | Plag. |
|---|---|---|
| S¹ Martin Ludgate | 4 | 4 |
| S¹ Martin Organs | 3 | 3 |
| S¹ Martin Outwitch | — | — |
| S¹ Martin Vintrey | 17 | 17 |
| S¹ Matthew Fridaystreet | — | — |
| S¹ Maudlin Milkstreet | 2 | — |
| S¹ Maudlin Oldfishstreet | 8 | 4 |
| S¹ Michael Basishaw | 12 | 11 |
| S¹ Michael Cornhill | — | — |
| S¹ Michael Crookedlane | 3 | 2 |
| S¹ Michael Queenhithe | 7 | 6 |
| S¹ Michael Queen | — | 1 |
| S¹ Michael Royal | — | 1 |
| S¹ Michael Woodstreet | 2 | 1 |
| S¹ Mildred Breadstreet | — | — |
| S¹ Mildred Poultrey | 4 | 1 |
| S¹ Nicholas Acons | — | — |
| S¹ Nicholas Coleabby | — | 1 |
| S¹ Nicholas Olaves | 3 | 1 |
| S¹ Olave Hartstreet | 2 | 2 |
| S¹ Olave Jewry | 4 | 3 |
| S¹ Olave Silverstreet | 23 | 22 |
| S¹ Pancras Soperlane | — | — |
| S¹ Peter Cheap | 1 | — |
| S¹ Peter Cornhill | 7 | 5 |
| S¹ Peter Paulswharf | 7 | 5 |
| S¹ Peter Poor | 2 | — |
| S¹ Steven Colemanstreet | 15 | 11 |
| S¹ Steven Walbrook | — | — |
| S¹ Swithin | — | — |
| S¹ Thomas Apostles | 8 | 7 |
| Trinity Parish | 5 | 5 |

Christned in the 97 Parishes within the Walls — 54   Buried — 538   Plague — 366

| | Bur. | Plag. | | Bur. | Plag. |
|---|---|---|---|---|---|
| S¹ Andrew Holborn | 421 | 220 | S¹ Botolph Aldgate | 228 | 112 | S¹ Saviour Southwark | 160 | 120 |
| S¹ Bartholomew Great | 58 | 50 | S¹ Botolph Bishopsgate | 355 | 236 | S¹ Sepulchres Parish | 405 | 274 |
| S¹ Bartholomew Lesse | 19 | 15 | S¹ Dunstan West | 26 | 19 | S¹ Thomas Southwark | 47 | 30 |
| S¹ Bridget | 147 | 119 | S¹ George Southwark | 80 | 60 | Trinity Minories | 8 | 5 |
| Bridewel Precinct | 7 | 5 | S¹ Giles Cripplegate | 847 | 572 | At the Pesthouse | 9 | 9 |
| S¹ Botolph Aldersgate | 70 | 61 | S¹ Olave Southwark | 225 | 131 | | | |

Christned in the 16 Parishes without the Walls — 61   Buried, and at the Pesthouse — 2861   Plague — 2119

| | Bur. | Plag. | | Bur. | Plag. |
|---|---|---|---|---|---|
| S¹ Giles in the fields | 304 | 175 | Lambeth Parish | 13 | 9 | S¹ Mary Islington | 50 | 45 |
| Hackney Parish | 13 | 8 | S¹ Leonard Shoreditch | 253 | 168 | S¹ Mary Whitechappel | 319 | 270 |
| S¹ James Clerkenwel | 172 | 171 | S¹ Magdalen Bermondsey | 57 | 36 | Rotherith Parish | — | 13 |
| S¹ Kath. near the Tower | 230 | 134 | S¹ Mary Newington | 74 | 73 | Stepney Parish | 371 | 173 |

Christned in the 12 out Parishes in Middlesex and Surrey — 49   Buried — 1571   Plague — 1144

| | Bur. | Plag. | | Bur. | Plag. |
|---|---|---|---|---|---|
| S¹ Clement Danes | 94 | 78 | S¹ Martin in the fields | 259 | 193 | S¹ Margaret Westminster | 210 | 191 |
| S¹ Paul Covent Garden | 28 | 16 | S¹ Mary Savoy | 13 | 10 | Parish of the Pesthouse | — | 13 |

Christned in the 5 Parishes in the City and Liberties of Westminster — 27   Buried — 598   Plague — 488

---

## The Diseases and Casualties this Week.

| | | | | |
|---|---|---|---|---|
| Abortive | — | | Impostume | 8 |
| Aged | 45 | | Infants | 22 |
| Bleeding | — | | Kingsevil | 4 |
| Broken legge | — | | Lethargy | 1 |
| Broke her scull by a fall in the street at St. Mary Woolchurch | 1 | | Livergrown | 1 |
| | | | Meagrome | 1 |
| | | | Palsie | 1 |
| Childbed | 28 | | Plague | 4237 |
| Chrisomes | 9 | | Purples | — |
| Consumption | 126 | | Quinsie | 5 |
| Convulsion | 89 | | Rickets | 23 |
| Cough | 1 | | Riting of the Lights | 18 |
| Dropsie | 53 | | Rupture | 1 |
| Feaver | 348 | | Scurvy | 3 |
| Flox and Small-pox | 11 | | Shingles | 1 |
| Flux | — | | Spotted Feaver | 166 |
| Frighted | 2 | | Stilborn | 2 |
| Gout | — | | Stone | 2 |
| Grief | 3 | | Stopping of the stomach | 17 |
| Griping in the Guts | 79 | | Strangury | — |
| Head-mould-shot | — | | Suddenly | 1 |
| Jaundies | 7 | | Surfeit | 74 |
| | | | Teeth | 111 |
| | | | Thrush | — |
| | | | Tissick | 9 |
| | | | Ulcer | — |
| | | | Vomiting | 10 |
| | | | Winde | 2 |
| | | | Wormes | — |

Christned { Males — 90, Females — 81, In all — 171 }   Buried { Males — 2777, Females — 2791, In all — 5568 }   Plague — 4237

Increased in the Burials this Week — 249

Parishes clear of the Plague — 27    Parishes Infected — 103

The Assize of Bread set forth by Order of the Lord Maior and Court of Aldermen,
A penny Wheaten Loaf to contain Nine Ounces and a half, and three
half-penny White Loaves the like weight.

A Rod for Run-awayes,
## Gods Tokens,
Of his fearefull Iudgements, sundry wayes pronounced vpon this City, and on seuerall persons, both flying from it, and staying in it.

*Expressed in many dreadfull Examples of sudden Death, falne vpon both young and old, within this City, and in the Suburbes, in the Fields, and open Streets, to the terrour of all those who liue, and to the warning of those who are to dye, to be ready when God Almighty shall bee pleased to call them.*

*By* T h o. D.

Lord, haue mercy on London.

I follow. We fly.

Wee dye. Keepe out.

Printed at London for *Iohn Trundle*, and are to be sold at his Shop in Smithfield. 1625.

"A ROD FOR RUN-AWAYES"

The title page of one of Thomas Dekker's plague pamphlets, 1625. The plague was almost continually present in London until late in the seventeenth century, but in some years, the so-called plague years, the disease broke out in a violent epidemic; 1625 was one of these plague years. In his pamphlet, "A Rod for Run-awayes," Dekker describes the conditions in London during the epidemic. The illustration on the title page shows the wrath of God descending as lightning from the clouds, and in the center death stands represented as a skeleton. On the left are men and women dead in the fields and over them is the inscription, "Wee dye"; on the right is a group of people fleeing from the plague and in response to their words, "Wee fly," death answers with, "I follow." The people of the suburban districts realized the truth of death's "I follow" and attempted to prevent the infected Londoners from contaminating their towns, as is shown by the armed men marked with the inscription, "Keep out."

*The exodus of people from towns during times of plague often disrupted provision for the sick and the implementation of measures to limit the spread of the disease. This illustration of 1625 attacks those who attempt to seek refuge away from the cities.*

Nevertheless, the reality was that the authorities (or those who remained) were powerless to halt the tide of fleeing refugees. Indeed, they were even unable to enforce the house quarantines in effect. The number of those locked at home was too great for their needs to be met, so many simply went out to find food. The number of hospital beds (about 8,500) available for the afflicted had been proven completely inadequate for the scale of the disaster. Few were surprised by this as the city had never made adequate provision for a possible outbreak despite the regular return (every fifteen to twenty years) of the epidemic.

With all these failings and the haemorrhage of wealthy trained citizens it was hardly a shock to learn that the death toll rose steeply throughout August. In the first week, 39,200 deaths were reported.

The following week saw nearly 8,000 deaths per day (54,600 in total). No one expected a respite as the hot weeks of August continued, since everyone knew that plague usually worsened in the late summer. Thus, the death of 59,500 people in the third week and a further 85,400 in the final week of August, while horrific, was not surprising. Final official figures reported that 313,600 Londoners had died in August and, of these, 238,700 deaths were attributed to the epidemic.

The scale of the burden placed on individual parts of the city was immense. The number of ill meant that many people, especially in working-class areas were, at least in theory, confined to their homes. Few people were willing to move about London in any case. Business was severely disrupted. More importantly, the production and distribution of foodstuffs became a serious problem, and there were reports that some people, while quarantined in their houses, simply starved to death. The sheer number of dead bodies also presented local officials with a tremendous problem. For obvious reasons, there was a desire to treat the dead with respect and their relatives with consideration. However, by the height of the epidemic in late summer, authorities were forced to resort to emergency procedures. Many open areas were converted into cemeteries as the available ones had become full. Two areas near Blackfriars had to dispose of over 42,000 bodies in August, and north of the Tower over 15,000 people were buried in a single mass grave. 'Plague pits' became all too common, as the number of dead mounted.

Official figures released throughout September showed, as expected, that the pestilence was worsening, although moments of hope did appear. The first week had over 14,000 deaths per day (98,000 total). In the face of this increase, the city ordered that every street be fumigated in an effort to destroy the pestilence. Although few would have credited the fumigation with success, in the second week there was a minor decline to only 91,700 deaths. Any chance that this might be a sign of the imminent cessation of the disease disappeared in the third week when plague deaths reached their highest point with 100,100 fatalities announced by the state. There was a significant decline in the last week of the month with only 77,700 deaths reported. Thereafter, the pestilence began to abate, October starting with 60,900 dead in the first week but dropping to only 14,700 by the last week of the month. November and December combined to record a further 57,400 deaths.

The final death toll was staggering. Reported deaths in the peri-od December to December were placed at nearly 1.4 million. Of these, official statistics listed nearly 1 million fatalities from the pestilence. However, there is every reason to think that there had been a significant under-reporting, both of the actual number of deaths themselves and of the number caused by the epidemic. For obvious reasons, many people preferred to bury their dead without notifying the authorities. This prevented the threat of quarantine and, especially in August and September, saved the deceased from the ignominy of being buried in a 'pit'. In addition, the general col-lapse of the governmental apparatus in the summer meant that many deaths simply went uncounted. The best estimates suggest that over 400,000 plague deaths went unreported. Consequently, the actual number of total deaths was nearer 1.8 million (on average 150,000 per month or nearly 5,000 per day). The number of plague deaths was probably slightly over 1.4 million of this total (nearly 117,000 per month or slightly under 4,000 per day).

❖        ❖        ❖

At this point, readers must be advised of two important points when reviewing the account of the plague outbreak above. First, the numbers have been altered to present the scale of the epidemic in a modern setting. In actual fact, the total population of London in 1665 was about 500,000. The present population of the city is slightly over 7 million. The estimated total number of deaths in 1665 is about 130,000, of which perhaps 100,000 were from plague. The official reported figures give a total of 97,306 dead with 68,596

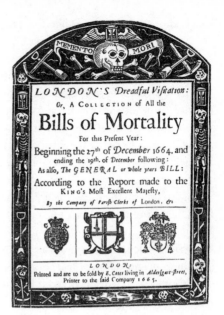

*The title page from a typical Bill of Mortality. Statistical accounts of plague made it possible for magistrates without medical training to identify patterns of mortality that might herald the onset of plague.*

deaths attributed to plague. Although even these numbers will surprise modern readers, the statistics have been given a modern setting in an effort to help the reader comprehend the scale of the disaster that the capital faced in 1665. The impact of an epidemic, no matter how many or few died, can only really be understood in relation to the total population. London was, and is, one of the largest cities in the world. In 1665, the city faced the death of 20 per cent of its population. Flight alone probably kept the total figure lower. One must remember that the total number of deaths was from a population much reduced by the migration of many citizens to other areas of the country. Had the entire population of 500,000 remained in the city after early June, the death toll would undoubtedly have been much, much greater.

While the first issue presented here to the reader is, in truth, no more than a literary conceit created purely for effect, the second is much more important. Other than the figures, the details given above are accurate for the 1665 outbreak. Many officials, including the clergy, fled the city. The plague was most acute in the poorer, more densely-populated parts of the city. By June, the Crown, the court, the legal profession, the parliament and the aristocracy had left the city for healthier parts of the country. Many parishes were forced to resort to communal mass graves. Some quarantined citizens probably did starve, since the system and workers charged with providing for their needs were inadequate to the task. The Council was unwilling to raise local taxes or rates to meet the emergency, preferring instead to rely on the money it already had coming in and donations from the rest of the country. The 600 spaces in London's five plague hospitals were woefully insufficient for any epidemic, as was widely recognised before, during and after the outbreak.

When plague deaths had first been reported in April, the state should not have been taken by surprise. There had been five isolated deaths the previous year, which had resulted in a strict quarantine on shipping entering the capital. Moreover, there was clear evidence that a more general outbreak was in the process of moving across the Continent. In 1661, plague was reported in the Ottoman Empire. By 1663-64, the disease had reached the Dutch Republic (with which England was at war) and killed approximately 35,000 in Amsterdam alone. Thus, everyone should have been on alert that plague was at the very doorstep of the country. Indeed, the presence of many prisoners of war (mostly Dutch sailors) from a region so recently struck with pestilence had every possibility of introducing the disease to England.

However, when the first plague deaths were reported at St Giles-in-the-Field, no real provisions had been made beyond vague attempts to re-state previous ordinances. A plague hospital was raised in Marylebone to treat the infected – another sign that the government recognised the inadequacy of the pre-existing five pest houses for dealing with any widespread outbreak. On 21 June 1665, the mayor attempted to seal off the whole of the parish to staunch the spread of the infection. At the same time, the number of infected overwhelmed the hospitals, forcing, as usual, the confinement of the ill at home. Their doors were marked with red crosses and the words 'Lord have mercy upon us'. Healthcare workers who had contact with the confined (or ill anywhere) were to carry four feet long white sticks so that passers-by would see them coming.

June saw concerted attempts to empty both the city, in general, and specific sites within the city, in particular. Innkeepers were ordered to expel lodgers, the theatres were closed, the courts and Inns of Court were closed, and the city's schools were ordered to suspend classes until the end of September. The Privy Council re-stated ordinances that were in keeping with the best practices developed in Italy over two centuries before. The order to remove lodgers, beggars and strangers (foreigners) was designed to ease overcrowding and, more importantly, to expel poorer people, who were seen as especially vulnerable to the plague and as likely sources of infection. The state ordered the ditches to be cleansed and public latrines removed from the main thoroughfares. Specific regulations were issued to control animals in the city. Stray cats and dogs were to be exterminated, domestic animals (hogs, pigeons and rabbits) were either to be contained closely or removed altogether. Industry was to remove sources of bad smells (contributors to miasma) such as musty corn, fish, and tanning. There was even a requirement that bakers keep hot bread in the bake-houses until the loaves had cooled and the odour dissipated. Most importantly of all, clothes (especially used clothes) were not to be sold or displayed publicly. The cloth was seen as porous enough to retain the poisonous, pestilence-bearing air and used clothes might well have come from dead plague victims.

Samuel Pepys (1633-1703), who remained in the city more or less throughout the outbreak, recorded in his diaries that many of the wealthier citizens began to move out of London. The exodus, however, was not general. For obvious reasons, the poor had no option but to stay. As Hooper, the Bishop of Gloucester, had said during an outbreak in the 1550s: 'there be certain persons that cannot flee although they would: as the poorer sort of people that have no friends nor place to flee unto, more than the poor house they dwell in [where they must stay]'. Those who could flee did not always do so. Many 'men of substance' sent away their wives and children, but stayed to look after their financial interests. Others, such as Pepys, might withdraw to homes or hamlets close enough to London to allow a daily commute into the capital. Thus, the refugees were often women, children and (superfluous) domestic servants. Pepys also noted that the behaviour of those who remained altered, and for the worse. He thought people were more cruel and heartless, not only to those whom they did not know, but also to those whom they did.

The most obvious example of the cruelty and heartlessness of men for their fellows was the flight of many clergy. The Bishop of London threatened to sack any that left their parishes. His concern,

*A broadsheet called* London's Lamentation *(1641) showing that whereas plague victims in London were taken from their beds and given a seemly burial, in the countryside victims fell by the wayside and were dragged by their feet to the nearest ditch.*

and that of the government, was twofold. Clearly, they were distressed to think that the people who remained would be without the benefit of clerical guidance and support. Their greater concern, though, was that non-conformist ministers would step into the resulting vacuum and undermine the established Church. One must remember that the Crown was only just restored and many Presbyterian ministers who had served London parishes faithfully and popularly had only recently been ejected from these same pulpits. They were ready and willing to return to their congregations. In the absence of established clergy and many supporters of the state, there was a general fear that these ministers might use the crisis as an opportunity for raising the people against the Crown and the episcopacy.

The confinement of the ill, the hospitals, the quarantine of ships, and the sealing of parishes were all very reactive measures intended to prevent the further spread of the disease. However, some felt that the epidemic could be driven from the town and their homes. Most still believed that plague was caused by infected air (that is, diseased airborne 'atoms' which could move about and 'stick' to various objects before infecting people). Animals, which freely wandered the streets and entered homes, were seen as a grave threat. No one knew where they had been and their coats were an ideal place for the miasmic air to adhere to. Dogs and cats, especially those that were not house pets, were ordered destroyed. Pets, such as the lapdogs of the wealthy, were exempted because they were confined to one place and unlikely to have had contact with infected areas. Stray animals were not so lucky. St Margarets (Westminster) reported the destruction and burial of 353 dogs alone. The city's official dog-catcher was paid for killing 4,380 dogs.

Both the Corporation and individuals also took action to attack the miasma directly rather than simply trying to prevent its transportation throughout the city, whether by people or animals. Pepys and others commented on the most common personal preventative employed by individuals: tobacco. Many smoked or chewed tobacco almost continuously and certainly when in the streets or in company. The Privy Council recommended the widespread use of a fumigant made of brimstone, saltpetre and amber. The Dean of St Pauls, William Sancroft (1617-93), fumigated his house with a mixture of brimstone, hops, pepper and frankincense. These fumigants were expensive and could only be used by the wealthy or, if by the state, as a last resort. In September, London's leaders decided that drastic action had to be taken. A few physicians argued that this practice was a 'showy and expensive' activity because the air was not actually infected. However, the most widely held opinion still supported miasma and so street fires were ordered. Tar barrels were set for every twelve houses and guards ordered to keep them burning even at night. The smells (whether good or bad) were supposedly strong enough to cleanse the air. For three days and nights the fires were kept burning until a heavy downpour put them out. The costs were extreme with parishes paying between three and a half pounds to over five pounds to maintain the fires. A similar rationale (relating to the effectiveness of strong smells) explains the order to open all of London's cesspools so that the stench could overwhelm the pestilential miasma.

Fortunately for the city, London was not left to bear the brunt of the epidemic itself. Although most of the government, officials and wealthy had fled, they were able to assist their fellow citizens at a distance by donations of money. Indeed, national appeals were able to raise the significant amount of over £7,600 in the period from July to December. Some parishes were able to rely on locals (and others) for large sums as well; for example, St Margarets (Westminster) received over £1,600 in bequests. Money was an essential part of the response to the epidemic. Not only did medicine and fumigants require money, but also those in the pest houses or sealed at home had to be fed. In addition, the dead had to be collected and buried. More prosaically, those who killed stray animals, buried them, watched the sealed houses, identified the afflicted and provisioned them all had to be paid. Since the Corporation refused to raise rates, money became a serious issue in the fight against the pestilence. By August, the lack of funds for meeting the most basic needs of those confined at home forced St Giles (Cripplegate) to let people leave their houses 'least the sick and poore should be famished within dores'. An even more basic problem than money was the length of the summer nights. By decree, burials were supposed to take place at night. The quantity of bodies and the lack of darkness forced this procedure to be abandoned. At every level, those responsible for containing the disease had to face manifold difficulties entirely separate from those actually infected.

One of the most important features of an outbreak, whether before, during or after, was the need to explain the cause of the mass mortality. Over 300 years after the first appearance of the Black Death in Europe, most, if not all, people continued to see plague as an act of God. Thus, the primary cause (the source, if one will) was known by common agreement. The important question that had to be answered was the reason why God had sent the plague. The appearance of plague was not a purely natural event, nor was it an arbitrary act of the Deity. God sent the plague against a particular society for a specific reason or set of reasons, which had to be identified. If the behaviour likely to cause plague could be removed (as the disease approached from other towns), then the pestilence might be avoided entirely. Once plague arrived, it was essential both to remove its cause and to appease an angered God. Finally, as plague began to abate in the winter months, it became crucial to prevent its return by identifying and eradicating those sins that had first evoked the Divine wrath.

The outbreak in London was no different; people needed to understand the cause of God's anger. The established Anglican Church had a simple explanation. With the events of the Civil War, the Protectorate and the Restoration so fresh in all minds, it was easy to decide that the cause of God's wrath was the continuing vestiges of the previous disturbed times. Thus, resistance to authority (non-conformity, anti-monarchical sentiments) was the cause of the plague. The *Form of Common Prayer* linked the advent of plague to disobedience, with a reference to the plagues (mentioned in chapter one) that had struck the Israelites for their disloyalty to Aaron and Moses. The state had to act to contain these contagious ideas to prevent the appearance or continuation of the medical contagion. For example, Quakers, the bugbear of the establishment, were arrested and jailed in Newgate and prison ships – seventy-nine died during their imprisonment. It was somewhat harder to explain the death of one third of the troops stationed in Hyde Park or the fifty-eight who fell ill in the Tower. More annoying was the fact that the clergy, who fled rather than lambasting their congregations for disobedience, were joined in their migration by many military officers. Some ministers who remained also stressed that the plague might be caused by sins other than resistance to the will of the magistrates and clergy. Hence, Thomas Plume, vicar of Greenwich, mentioned the plague-causing powers of fornication, uncleanness, inordinate affections, lust, covetousness and idolatry.

Despite the well-founded fear that the plague would reappear in 1666, the disease seemed to have burnt itself out. By 1 February, the King was able to return to the city. The final cost of the pestilence was immense – the plague had taken a reported 68,596 lives. However, this number is surely the minimum. In addition to those deaths intentionally hidden (or whose cause was misreported), it is clear that some groups were not counted in the figures that had been compiled, for the most part, by parish officials. Jewish, Quaker and other non-conformist deaths probably went unreported and unremarked. Moreover, these overall figures hide the extent to which the plague deaths were unevenly distributed around the city. The poorer parishes of the city suffered a much higher death toll, both in raw numbers and as a percentage of their populations. For example, the parishes south of the Thames, including Southwark, seem to have lost 30 per cent of the populace compared to the city-wide average of 20 per cent. Wealthier parishes were only mildly hit – within the city walls (especially around the prosperous Cheapside district), only 5 per cent of the people appear to have died. One should not necessarily assume (as did the people of the time) that wealth was, in and of itself, a prophylactic. Rather, the ability of the rich to flee the city meant that during the outbreak the actual number of people in the wealthier districts was considerably reduced. That is, fewer rich died because there were fewer around to catch the plague.

❖      ❖      ❖

Although many might assume that the Great Plague of London was an isolated event, this was clearly not the case. Not only did the outbreak strike many places across the Continent, but also many other parts of England. Indeed, some cities suffered much more severely (as a proportion of their populations) than London. Nevertheless, the plague in London stands out in the memory of most people as a singular event, almost in a vacuum. It is important, therefore, to place the pestilence in the capital in its wider context. Nor was the 1665 plague unique. Early modern London had been struck by other outbreaks just as costly. The worst were in 1563, 1603 and 1625, with lesser (though still important epidemics) in 1578, 1582, 1593 and 1636. Thus, there is a chronological context to the 1665 outbreak, as well as a geographical one needing some discussion.

The first areas to fall victim to the pestilence after London were the smaller towns and villages lying near to the capital. Refugees seem to have spread the plague as they fled. In Hampstead, 260 deaths were reported out of a normal population of 800. The mortality rate of 32.5 per cent is misleading as the town was probably swollen with refugees. Nevertheless, the deaths would have had a dramatic impact on so small a locale. Other outlying areas were struck: 122 dead at Kingston-upon-Thames, 432 at Brentford, 245 at Wandsworth, 200 at Barking and 109 at Romford.

Further afield, the epidemic continued its relentless march. The quartering of Dutch prisoners and their guards in various towns did

*A tally of the number of deaths by parish in Norwich during one week of plague in 1666.*

not alleviate the difficulties faced by urban areas as they struggled to prevent or contain the plague. This meant that many towns were overburdened with prisoners, soldiers and refugees. It is, therefore, difficult accurately to discuss the proportional impact of the plague on any given town, as it is almost impossible to estimate the actual number of people endangered by the approach of the pestilence. Thus, while we know that 5,345 people died in Colchester during the period 14 August 1665-14 December 1666, and that 4,817 of these were ascribed to plague, we cannot necessarily be assured that the total exposed was only the normal population of 11,000. Assuming, however, that some of Colchester's resident citizenry would have fled, the figures of 49 per cent overall dead and 44 per cent from plague certainly indicate that the plague was much more severe in its impact on Colchester than London. Moreover, the period of the deaths highlights the fact that the epidemic in London was confined to 1665, while areas outside the capital tended to be struck later in 1665 and re-infected in 1666.

The two rounds of plague (in late 1665 and much of 1666) battered many of the nation's major cities and towns. Norwich, the largest provincial city, with 20,000 inhabitants, suffered a total of 3,682 (18 per cent) deaths of which 2,810 (14 per cent) were from plague. As in London, this overall figure hides the skewing of the deaths to poorer areas. Poor parishes had three times the mortality rate of wealthier areas. Southampton was so badly affected by the epidemic in 1665-66 that the parochial registration system completely collapsed and accurate figures were not kept. So many of the

*A record of the number of deaths in the town and parish of Great Yarmouth during February 1665. It shows that there were three deaths – ascribed as 'aged', 'infant' and 'death' – but, as the clerk noted, not one of them was due to plague.*

town's clergy and officials fled that some baptisms and marriages had to be performed by the minister of the French Huguenot church, creating the ironic situation whereby the people of Southampton were spiritually cared for by the refugees of French religious persecution. Their own native ministers had made themselves plague refugees. After the epidemic subsided, the mayor and a further sixteen magistrates were fined for abandoning their posts during the crisis.

The plague had additional repercussions. As has already been mentioned, education was severely disrupted with Cambridge breaking up in summer 1665 and, after a brief attempt to restart the following spring, ending classes again in June 1666. Other effects of the pestilence are more surprising now and, at the time, considerably more frightening. In Portsmouth, infected people were accused of throwing their plasters into the windows of healthy homes. Was this perhaps an attempt to attack the rich? Certainly, some of those confined in Portsmouth did break their quarantine and invade the houses of the wealthy. In the end, armed troops had to be used to bring the situation under control with the death of one protestor and the wounding of three others. It was even reported in London (Westminster) that sick people leaned out of their windows and breathed on passers-by.

Many cities attempted to stop the pestilence from breaching their walls by preventing the entry of Londoners or anyone travelling from any other infected area. Indeed, the Scottish Privy Council followed the English example of banning Dutch trade in 1664, and followed this with bans on contact with London and other infected areas in England during July 1665. This use of exclusion (and its close cousin, quarantine) was simply a part of the raft of regulations and ordinances developed in Italy in the fifteenth century. Thus, Winchester set watches on its gates, ordered sanitary regulations for 'the cleanlyness, decency and sweetness of the eyre' and cancelled the mayor's dinner and other festivals. Bristol and Exeter ordered their guards to prevent the entry of anyone from London. Although severe, the national outbreak varied in its intensity quite dramatically. Some areas (for example, the west of England and Wales) were lightly affected, if at all, while some towns (Colchester, Braintree and Southampton) seem to have lost nearly 50 per cent of their residents to the disease. Of those cities affected, places like Salisbury (with about 500 deaths from 7,000 or 7 per cent) were on one end of the scale with Colchester at the other extreme. London, with a mortality rate estimated at 20 per cent, was probably fairly typical.

Of the outbreaks in the provinces, only one is widely known to modern readers. When plague first struck the village of Eyam, the rector (William Mompesson, 1639-1709) and his predecessor (Thomas Stanley) were determined to prevent the spread of the disease to neighbouring communities. They convinced the entire village to abide by a strict quarantine. In effect, the villagers sealed themselves in. The Earl of Devonshire agreed to ensure that the villagers were supplied with necessary victuals. Supplies were left by outsiders and collected by the villagers from a no-man's land. Anything from the village (for example, money) was placed in a trough of water, so that the uninfected might collect it cleansed. In the end, this extreme quarantine seems to have been successful. The epidemic did not spread. However, Eyam suffered a mortality rate of 30 per cent from a population of about 950. At least seventy-five homes suffered at least one death.

❖     ❖     ❖

Why is the London plague so well known? Why is it treated as a singular event and not in its wider geographical and chronological context when the rest of England was also affected? The 1665 outbreak was but one of many. A number of explanations for this can be given. First, the body of documentation, particularly of a literary nature, relating to the London plague is crucial. Pepys' diary plays an important part in this. However, Daniel Defoe's *A Journal of the Plague Year* is probably more important. Although not an eyewitness account, Defoe (1660-1731) managed to bring the plague to life in a very dramatic form. His work made many people very aware indeed of the details of the outbreak. Also, the importance of the capital and the extreme loss of life (in actual numbers) were dramatic and memorable almost to the exclusion of experiences elsewhere. Only little Eyam, with its self-sacrificing quarantine, has been able to break the monopolistic hold of the metropolis on the popular memory.

Not only has the London plague of 1665 managed to grab the popular imagination and to stand out as a seemingly unique piece of cultural history, but it has also produced a number of myths. The first relates again to Defoe. Although his account is probably accurate with regard to the spirit of the event, it is fictional. For most people, though, it is so familiar and has so defined the popular perception of the plague that many are unaware that it is a piece of literature, not history. Second, as has been hinted above, the belief in miasma (much derided by modern folk) was not universally held. There were some who rejected the traditional interpretation so succinctly expressed by John Graunt in his *Natural and Political Observations*: 'the Contagion of the Plague depends more upon the Disposition of the Air [miasma]; than upon the effluxia from the Bodies of men [contagion]'. The opponents of this view insisted upon a diagnosis that stressed the contagious nature of the disease. The debate between miasma and contagion was not new and supporters of the contagion theory had been a significant minority since the first appearance of the Black Death. More importantly, by 1665, there were many who argued that chemicals, not sweet-smelling herbs, were the best treatment for pestilence. Indeed, the Society of Chemical Physicians set themselves up in 1665 in opposition to the Royal College of Physicians. Although their demands that the active ingredients of chemicals should be identified and used, along with treatment and diagnosis based on observation and experimentation (rather than theory and philosophy), eventually won the argument, the society collapsed shortly after its inception. Finally, the popular belief that the Great London Fire of 1666 ended the disease is patently incorrect. Clearly, the destruction of over 13,000 homes and nearly ninety churches was a disaster of tremendous proportions; however, the plague had actually ended nearly nine months before.

One feature of the 1665 outbreak is important, inasmuch as it was part of the wider 1664-67 plague in England – namely that it was the last outbreak in England. Obviously, no one at the time could – or would – have thought that this would be the last plague to strike the nation. In fact, there was every reason to expect that the plague would return to the capital or the nation (or some part thereof) in the following fifteen or twenty years. Past experience led most people to expect that the period 1680-85 would see yet another cycle of epidemics in any number of cities and towns, but these failed to materialise. As time went by, the memory of the London outbreak became the final, and enduring, memory of the plague. However, people continued to fear the return of the disease and, in the late eighteenth and early nineteenth century, when diseases such as yellow fever appeared, many Europeans thought these might actually be plague under an altered or mutated guise. To understand the enduring and traumatic legacy of a disease that last struck over three centuries ago, it is critical to understand the sweep of plague in the history of England.

Obviously, plague first struck in the form of the Black Death around 1350. In the period 1348-1485, England was struck by eighteen major national outbreaks (an average of one every seven to eight years). In 1410-40, Colchester was afflicted nine times (every three years); Canterbury (1413-1517) had thirteen plagues (every eight years); Norwich suffered severe outbreaks in 1579-80, 1584-5 and 1589-92. In 1589-91, a number of rural Devonshire parishes recorded a mortality rate five times above the annual norm. The mechanism for coping with pestilence gained a great impetus in 1518 with royal decrees ordering that infected houses be marked by straw bundles and plague workers by white sticks. In addition, the Royal College of Physicians was founded. The following year, London began to produce *Bills of Mortality* listing the monthly number of deaths and their causes. By 1618, the city added a

Commission for New Buildings. Its creation was designed to control the sprawl of the growing metropolis, both to limit overcrowding and to provide some level of sanitation.

However, unlike Italy and many other nations on the Continent, the adoption of the best medical and sanitary practices was not universal in England, especially in London. The century separating the establishment of the Royal College and the Commission for Buildings is dramatic and instructive. In 1578 (and again in 1604), the Corporation of the City of London gained exemption from national plague prevention legislation. To limit the financial impact of home confinement, one person could leave an infected house to get food for the other inmates. This avoided the need for an extensive and expensive system of workers to supply those sealed in their houses. This contrasts with York, where, from 1550, those quarantined were guaranteed a weekly stipend. London was also exempted from the imposition of a special tax (a plague rate) during outbreaks. Instead of forcing citizens to fund the healthcare of the city during a crisis, London's leaders preferred to rely on local and national charity, as well as normal taxation. The request, from the Privy Council in 1583, for a pest house was not answered with action until 1594 when construction actually began. In the end, the paucity of plague beds has already been noted.

Many regulations and responses to plague commonly seen on the Continent from the early sixteenth century (and earlier in Italy) did not appear in England until the early 1600s. In 1607 and 1610, the Privy Council moved to limit the production of starch (a very smelly process) from heavily-populated urban areas. In Hull (1606), fish livers were not to be kept or cured within a half-mile of the city. Because of plague in France and the Low Countries, ships from those regions were quarantined; this behaviour was repeated thereafter. More bizarre actions were also taken. For example, Bristol and Southampton banned the use of horse-drawn carts in the town centres to limit the spread of manure (and its stench); sledges had to be drawn through the streets by people instead. However, despite the best efforts of government, many regulations were ignored or circumvented. Thus, the Privy Council reprimanded London's medical workers for not enforcing the identification and confinement of the afflicted.

These ordinances and regulations were decreed and enforced against the backdrop of an endemic disease. It was obvious to most observers of the day that at some point in the early sixteenth century the plague had changed its cyclical pattern. For the first 150 years after the Black Death, the pestilence recurred approximately every decade. Thereafter, the attacks of the disease, though seemingly no less virulent, became less frequent. Plague visitations were now expected every twenty years. Although less frequent, the scale of death in a plague outbreak meant that the fear of pestilence and the desire to prevent it were not at all lessened. The mortality rates were extreme indeed. In 1600-70, over 2 million French died of the epidemic (from a population that was never able to exceed 12 million). In 1629-32, over 35,000 people died in Lyons alone. In the 1630s, half the population of Venice succumbed; a similar ratio died in Genoa (1656-57). The Italian town of Pescia was spared so high a mortality in 1631 when only one third of the people died. Londoners would have been well aware in 1665 that similar attacks had previously befallen the capital: 10,400 plague victims were buried in April-December 1636.

❖        ❖        ❖

Why was the outbreak of 1665 the last outbreak in England? The simple answer is that no adequate explanation has been advanced. Some have suggested that the Fire of London produced a change in buildings since many of the timber structures were replaced with stone. This rests on the presumption that rats were less likely (or able) to live near people in stone structures. The reality is that the structures were not substantially able to prevent the presence of rats. Others would propose changes in sanitation. Some hypothesise that the population was increasingly immune to the disease or that the plague bacillus had mutated into a less virulent form. The problem with almost every explanation is that the logical result would be a slow decline in the number of plague deaths. Rather, as in London, the disease ceased with an outbreak as virulent as almost any before. The plague did not slowly end as sanitation or immunity or mutation had an effect on its ability to kill. Instead, the disease roared across London and many other English cities, took thousands of lives and never returned.

Perhaps it is this final hurrah that has given the London plague such a hold on the popular imagination. One of the greatest killers ever to stalk England did not fade away, technology or medical science did not overcome it, nor did it succumb to an ever stronger human gene pool. Instead, the plague simply left, having proven its ability to kill on a grand scale. The Great Plague of London remains as a lasting and profound image of man's impotence in the face of nature. Pestilence was not defeated, prevented, or contained – it departed. London was left with empty homes and idle shops. Vast scars of brown earth scored the green fields as poignant yet fading monuments to the dead in their mass graves. The state and its officials had been revealed as powerless and cowardly. Whole families were exterminated and countless thousands of others were left to grieve for their losses. Death had not come on the battlefield or from visible disasters such as drought and flood. Rather, death had slipped quietly from one house to the other, through every street and alley, over every wall and barrier. The Great Plague of London stands out in the memory of people because the plague proved that it was able to bring mass death to a great metropolis and then to leave unscathed. That we are still unable to explain the sudden departure of the pestilence only adds to the mystique of the disease, and the monumental and iconic nature of the 1665 plague in London.

1 A seventeenth-century interpretation of the plague which befell the Philistines at Ashdod. The heretical beliefs of the Philistines were punished with two plagues: one of rats and mice to consume their food and the other a painful attack of piles to make their lives a misery.

2 The devastation caused by war (note the armies in the background), pestilence and famine, the latter being depicted by a mother feeding her children. Because of their ferocity, these were the three greatest dangers that could befall a community.

3 *Above:* Based on a work by Raphael, this engraving provides a Renaissance view of the plague in Phrygia. The artistic representation of plague in ancient and Biblical times served to place the medieval and early modern plague victims in a historical and modern context, stressing the continuity of reality and the human experience.

4 *Right:* The *Nuremberg Chronicle* was printed in the fifteenth century and included this account of the outbreak of plague in 1348.

5 These annotations were written at the bottom of a page of ancient Irish laws, attributed to St Patrick, and give an insight into the fears caused by the Black Death.

6 An English version of a treatise on plague written by Jean de Bourgogne, which he dates as 1365.

I non essent regultrantes
et futuris ministrantes que
vident et que audiunt.

que non viderunt nec sciunt
per scripturas edocemur
si nos bene recordemur. que sunt

7 *Above:* An illustration from the annals of Gilles de Muisit, showing the burial of plague victims at Tournai in 1349. It begins with the empty coffins in the top left-hand corner, showing the digging of graves in the middle and the burial of bodies in the bottom right-hand corner. However, during an epidemic, plague pits rather than individual graves would have been the norm.

8 *Right:* A Mass for the Dead, from a printed Book of Hours. Note the soul being carried away overhead.

Mortuorum. Fo. rcviij.

CONDEMNATVS SVM

RESPONDE MICHI

A chanon the whiche at Parys dyed
As they his seruyce in the quere dyde syng
At the fourth lesson alowde he cryed
Sayng I am dampned for my lyuyng.

9 An inscription from Ashwell church in Hertfordshire which states that in 1350: 'the deplorable, fierce, raging pestilence departed: the dregs of the people survived to tell the tale.' The second line refers to the return of the plague in 1361: 'At the end of the second visitation there was a mighty wind. Maurice [sic] thunders in the city.'

10 A watercolour of a wooden carving representing the clergy and people of Lyons calling upon God for deliverance from the plague in the fifteenth century. Just as God was the prime cause of plague, His ability to deliver people from the affliction was paramount. Only by appeasing God could plague be avoided or halted.

11 *Right:* A priest administers the last rites to a dying man while overhead an angel and God look down. From below the devil and a griffin await the hour of death.

12 *Below left:* Based on a mid-fifteenth-century painting by Bonfigli, this lithograph shows the Virgin Mary responding to the intercession of saints and protecting people from the arrows of disease, while below the devil stalks the plague-ravaged land.

13 *Below right:* An engraving by Dürer from 1510 of a flagellant whipping his body before the altar as punishment for his sins. In spite of official disapproval, such behaviour was common in the wake of the Black Death, as individuals punished themselves in order to assuage God's displeasure which had caused the plague.

¶ The ben in glory and worldly fauour
full of all welth / rychesse / and substaunce
But now we percepue that come is the houre
That we must leue all lust and pleasaunce

¶ We haue somtyme abyden our chaunce
In this worlde / passyng tyme lustely
But now ye must come trace on our daunce
All adams kynde be ordeyned to dye.

14 *Left:* For the skeletons who have shadowed the living through life, their time has come as the living (depicted as horsemen) are forced to give up a life of pleasure. The verses below emphasise the inevitability of death.

15 *Above left:* People attempted to protect themselves from the plague in various ways, including the use of talismans such as this one from a fifteenth-century leech book.

16 *Above right:* Taken from the same page of the *Nuremberg Chronicle* that narrates the arrival of the plague, this image shows the burning of the Jews. The Jewish community was often made a scapegoat for the spread of plague and disease.

17 England's first Sanitary Act, dating from 1388, in the reign of Richard II (1366–1400).

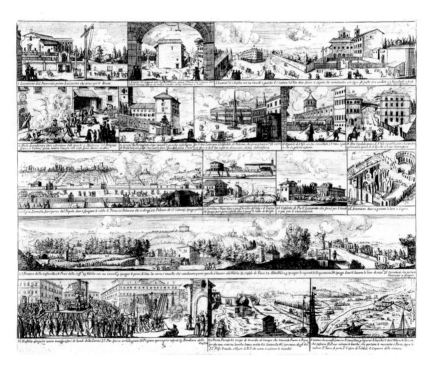

18 A pictorial broadsheet depicting the measures used to deal with the 1656 plague in Rome.

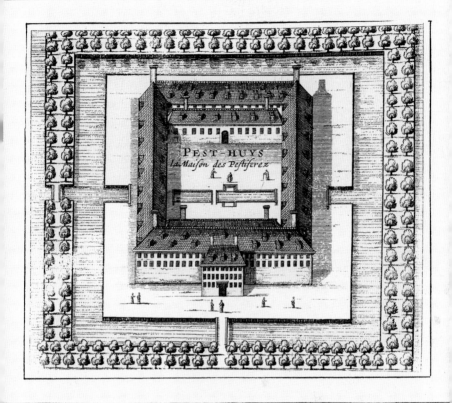

19 A bird's-eye view of the pest house at Leiden in the Netherlands, founded in the seventeenth century. The location and plan of a pest house were meant to isolate the infected while providing them with access to suitably sanitary and wholesome surroundings.

20 *Above left:* St Carlo Borromeo, Bishop of Milan, ministered to the city's plague victims during 1576. As a result he became another saint associated with the relief of plague.

21 *Above right:* The frontispiece of Thomson's *Loimotomia* on how to dissect a pestilential victim. Note the blotches on the body of the corpse and the steaming bowl beside it, used to dispel the 'miasma' held to cause plague.

22 *Left:* A wooden box from the seventeenth century used for collecting money for those suffering from the plague. The side of the box is carved with a relief depicting St Roch.

23 A funeral and burial from the late sixteenth or early seventeenth century. In the foreground a male corpse is wrapped prior to burial. In the background is a funeral procession with a coffin being borne into church.

24 A photograph of one of the pits used to bury victims of the plague in London during the 1660s.

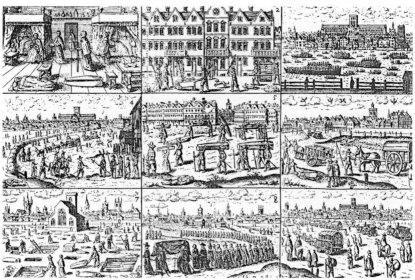

25 A broadsheet of 1665-6 showing the course of the London plague of 1665. As the disease starts in London, people begin to flee the city either by river or across the fields. For those who remain there is the constant process of burying the dead. In the churchyards mass pits are used but the ground is rapidly filled up – nonetheless, traditional funeral customs continue. In the final vignette the plague is over and people return to the city.

26 *Above left:* In 1742 a vault at St Botolph's Aldgate in London which had been closed at the time of the plague in 1665 was reopened. Inside were found the remains of a twelve-year-old boy.

27 *Above right:* A late seventeenth-century view of a barber-surgeon's shop, in which a number of people are being treated. On the wall behind are various tools of the trade.

28 *Left:* An angel descends on a French town in the seventeenth century with a sword bringing pestilence.

29 A plan of the *lazaretto* at Marseilles in the late eighteenth century, showing the area used for treating those suffering from plague (marked with a star, centre top) and other infectious diseases, as well as the different accommodation provided for the passengers in quarantine according to their social status. Note also the double perimeter wall.

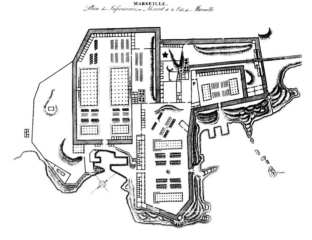

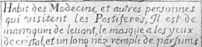

Habit des Medecins, et autres personnes qui visitent les Pestiferes, Il est de maroquin de levant, le masque a les yeux de cristal, et un long nez rempli de parfums

Abrib eines in Cordian Leeder bekleideten mit einem von Pest vertreibendem Rauchwerck angefüllten Rasten Futer versehenen Doctors von Marseille Der mit einem Stecken den Puls soll fühlen.

30 The dress of a doctor during the plague in Marseilles (*above left*) and a German caricature of the same doctor (*above right*).

31 Two contemporary scenes from Marseilles at the time of the plague of 1720, showing the Town Hall and harbour (*above*) and the view towards the plague hospital. The state of chaos is evidenced by the piles of bodies in the streets.

32 Views from a study by John Howard at the end of the eighteenth century of the principal *lazarettos* (buildings designed to treat those suffering from infectious diseases) in Europe. Above is the Health Office at the entrance to the port of Naples and, below, the *lazaretto* at Genoa (note its isolated location).

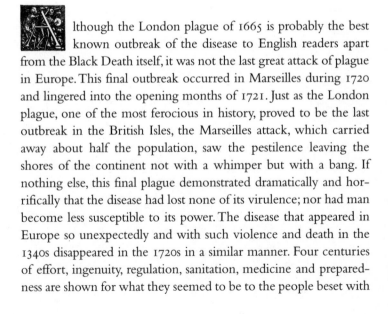

—◌ Six ◌—

# DEATH'S ENCORE
## The Marseilles Plague
### 1720

*Every house, every street, every alley, resounds with sighs and groans. Terror resides in every heart, and is stamped on every face.*

Dr Bertrand

lthough the London plague of 1665 is probably the best known outbreak of the disease to English readers apart from the Black Death itself, it was not the last great attack of plague in Europe. This final outbreak occurred in Marseilles during 1720 and lingered into the opening months of 1721. Just as the London plague, one of the most ferocious in history, proved to be the last outbreak in the British Isles, the Marseilles attack, which carried away about half the population, saw the pestilence leaving the shores of the continent not with a whimper but with a bang. If nothing else, this final plague demonstrated dramatically and horrifically that the disease had lost none of its virulence; nor had man become less susceptible to its power. The disease that appeared in Europe so unexpectedly and with such violence and death in the 1340s disappeared in the 1720s in a similar manner. Four centuries of effort, ingenuity, regulation, sanitation, medicine and preparedness are shown for what they seemed to be to the people beset with plague – futile. Plague departed from Europe mocking the best efforts of society, government and education. It continues to mock every effort to explain its departure by refusing to conform to any explanations advanced by the cleverness of modern historians, doctors and epidemiologists. The people of Marseilles, who were descended from a gene pool struck every eleven to fifteen years by plague for over 370 years, show no sign of having grown immune to the pestilence. The disease that carried away nearly 40 per cent of the city's population at its first appearance and 50 per cent at its last hardly demonstrates signs of having mutated into a less virulent form. London and Marseilles serve as the final calling cards of an epidemic that departed Europe – and remains – unbeaten and inexplicable.

While one might expect a bare recitation of the plague in Marseilles to follow, the city has actually left an important record that allows for a different approach. One of the city's leading physicians, who was intimately involved both in treating the disease and dealing with leading officials at the time, has left a detailed account of the progress of the epidemic. It is very rare that one can gain so clear an insight into the behaviour of those responsible for coping with a pestilential outbreak. Thus, it would seem useful to use this surviving work in order to study this outbreak from the inside. Dr Bertrand, who was born on 12 July 1670, was fifty years old when the plague struck Marseilles; he died on 10 September 1752. Although a native of a small village (Martiques) near the metropolis, he had moved to Marseilles and been inducted into its small, but very powerful, College of Physicians. This college, comprised of twelve physicians, was a self-perpetuating cartel. As such, they considered themselves the supreme font of medical knowledge in the city and were secured in this position by their monopoly on the provision of medicine to the wealthy of Marseilles.

It was to Marseilles that Dr Bertrand returned in 1707. He had previously studied theology in the city's Jesuit College in 1689. Originally tending towards the priesthood, he thence removed himself to Avignon. There he became friends with a physician and changed his career. After an initial tutelage under this doctor, Bertrand continued his studies at one of Europe's premier medical schools, Montpellier. Having completed his studies, he worked both in his hometown of Martiques and in Lyons. However, he eventually returned to Marseilles and was accepted into the College of Physicians as a Doctor of Medicine in 1708. He became one of the Marseilles' four 'physicians in ordinary', which meant that he was responsible for providing regular medical treatment to a specific quarter of the city. Among his many duties in this role was the inspection of corpses after suspicious deaths to ascertain if any epidemic disease might be present. As such, he was in a fortunate position to study the advance of the pestilence from its very inception.

The plague of 1720 was, as has already been said, extremely virulent. The best estimates are that about 50,000 people died from a population of 100,000. However, the mortality rate of 50 per cent is somewhat deceptive. Approximately 10,000 people fled the city at the first appearance of the disease. Thus, the deaths were from a human pool of about 90,000. This meant that about 56 per cent died and a further 11 per cent (10,000) were afflicted but recovered. This level of illness and mortality is on a par with the worst cases of the previous four centuries. Even more disturbing, the disease struck a city, as we shall see, that was extremely well prepared for coping with epidemic disease. The *lazaretto* (or plague quarantine hospital) was set off from the city. Measures were taken to quarantine everything and everyone coming from the East where plague was recognised as being endemic. The quarantine staff wore special jackets, pantaloons, gloves and shoes, which were either waxed or oiled to prevent the 'sticking' of any infected (miasmic) air particles.

Even when discussing the outbreak that proved to be Europe's last, Bertrand started by discussing the history of plague not only in Marseilles but also more generally. At the start, and in subsequent places in his account, the good doctor made mention of various

Biblical plagues, the plague in Athens, as well as diverse epidemics associated with the First Great Pandemic. For example, he noted times of mortality recounted by Gregory of Tours during 588 and 591 in Provence. However, he was more interested in recent outbreaks. In particular, Bertrand wanted to stress the gullibility of people faced with a pestilence. One of the themes of his work is the desire of people and officials to deny the presence of plague, to dismiss its virulence and to believe in simplistic curatives.

In 1580, the credulity of people, of all classes and educational levels, was most evident. In that year, a severe plague struck the town of Aix-en-Provence. Bertrand noted that 'scarcely a house was free from infection and whole families were destroyed by it'. The physicians and surgeons, knowing the extremity of the danger, refused to attend the sick. Into this calamitous situation came the 'Holy Hermit' (also called the 'Holy Father'). This man was dressed in a hair shirt, sandals and was girded by a belt with a crucifix and chaplet. He was the very image of an early modern Catholic John the Baptist. Since he had had the illness, he was immune and he had devoted himself to the care of the afflicted. Thus he combined the image of St Roch with John the Baptist. He wandered about supposedly curing many while preaching repentance. So popular was his reputation and so powerful his supposed abilities, an industry arose to produce pictures of the hermit. These were bought by many and used as talismans both to prevent and to cure the pestilence. Moreover, people rushed to kiss his garments and they erected altars to him as a living saint.

When plague returned to Provence in 1587, the hermit was called forth from his seclusion and consulted by officials in many places, including Lyons and Montelimar. However, as the disease spread and flourished, the people began to look for a cause. Eventually, suspicion fell on their previous saviour, the Holy Hermit. Physicians, who had greatly resented his work, quickly noticed that plague often appeared after an advisory visit from the man. They opined that he would deny the presence of the disease during its initial stages to allow it to take hold. This would give him the chance to return and work his wonders. Indeed, they claimed to have discovered that he was actively transporting the disease in infected items. Consequently, he was arrested and blamed for the pestilence, much as Jews had been in the fifteenth century and plague workers in the sixteenth.

After a lengthy trial, the hermit was exposed as a charlatan. He had used his visitations into private homes as an opportunity to make advances towards women. He was shown to have been previously accused of murder and to have deserted from the army. However, using his great powers of persuasion, he had managed to obtain a full absolution from Pope Gregory XIII (1502-85). Some even suggested that he had been paid by the King of Spain to spread the plague in southern France. In addition, although a Franciscan, he had married and, for a time, lived in a Protestant country. While he had been absolved, his dissolute past had led the Pope to forbid him from ever celebrating Mass. Finally, it was alleged that he and his mistress (Joan Arnaud) had intentionally infected towns and individuals to maintain the authoritative place he had acquired in society because of his alleged abilities. Eventually, the (by now) very unholy hermit was convicted and burnt alive while his mistress was flogged. Bertrand was left to muse that 'all honest people … could not help observing … how easily and how lamentably mankind may be duped by those who cover their villainy with a cloak of religion'.

Undoubtedly, the cessation of the plague very soon after the arrest of the hermit was seen as further proof of his guilt. Bertrand, however, said that the disease was ended by the severely cold winter of 1587-8. He also mentioned in passing other subsequent pestilences that struck Marseilles in 1630 and 1649-50, but his real interest was the 1720 outbreak. As any good physician of his day, or of the 400 years previous, Bertrand was at pains to explain the return of the plague. He reported that there were two major explanations advanced. First, many, if not most, still held to the traditional reason of miasma. Others, he said, sought to blame food for the disease. That is, they said that an abundance of (over)ripe fruit had caused people to sicken. Bertrand rejected both in favour of an explanation based on contagion. He said that the geographical situation of the city (near the sea) and its provision with many fountains and drains meant it was very clean. Also, the mountains were covered with sweet-smelling herbs. In addition, there had been no natural phenomena to upset the air, such as comets, meteors, earthquakes or volcanic eruptions. Bertrand did admit that the habit of dumping all waste, even human, into the streets was insanitary (as well as dangerous to those walking beneath the windows). However, the problem was not great as the 'peasants, eager for manure, so necessary for the fertilization of their lands' regularly and speedily removed the worst of the ordure. In short, Marseilles enjoyed a healthy location and was not given to even the most common and ordinary of diseases. Bertrand made short shrift of any problems with fruit, since he argued that this tended to promote good health rather than invite disease.

More important than the natural advantages present at Marseilles were the precautions taken by the government. As a major Mediterranean port, the city was in regular contact with the Middle East where, as everyone knew, plague was endemic. Consequently, every ship that arrived in the harbour was forced to endure quarantine. In normal circumstances, the crew was placed in the *lazaretto* and the cargo was unpacked and exposed to the fresh air. If a boat arrived showing any evidence of disease, the ship, crew and cargo were quarantined and cleansed on Jarre Island away from the city. Further, there was a committee of sixteen health officials (intendants) to serve Marseilles. The *lazaretto* was a sophisticated building placed at some distance from the city. It was built around a central court and surrounded by a high wall. After 1720, an additional wall was built to prevent anything being thrown across the single wall. The idea was that nothing suspected of disease would actually reach the mainland until after a period of quarantine. Even in the best circumstances, nothing would be moved from the area of the infirmary and into the city until after a period of observation had ensured that no disease in incubation was admitted to Marseilles. Bertrand was convinced that, had these precautions been followed as prescribed, the plague would never have been able to breach the city's health defences.

❖      ❖      ❖

When Captain Chataud sailed from Sidon on 31 January 1720, he did so with a clear conscience. He had on board a certificate stating that neither his crew nor cargo had come into contact with plague. He next landed at Tripoli, where he took on more cargo and some Turkish passengers who came from Cyprus. He there learned that plague had broken out in Sidon just days after his sailing. Since Islamic countries took no precautions against the disease, trade between Sidon and Tripoli had continued unabated. Chataud then put into Leghorn in Italy, where he reported the death at sea of one Turkish passenger and eleven sailors. The health officials at Leghorn noted on their health certificate that the ship was infected with a 'malignant, pestilential fever'. Under those circumstances, Chataud assumed that he would be quarantined at Jarre Island. However, despite having made the port officials aware of the situation on board when he arrived on 25 May, he was told to put in at the infirmary quay. His goods and crew were offloaded there. On 31 May, another three ships arrived from the Middle East and another on 12 June. Again, although having sailed from an infected region, the ships were quarantined on the shore at the *lazaretto*. The surgeon there examined the infected – including the one who died after arrival – and declared that Chataud's crew was suffering from a fever not the plague. He ordered a forty-day quarantine, commencing the day the last bale was offloaded. When more sailors, some shore porters and even one of the health officials died, the surgeon finally acted. He ordered everyone to remove themselves to Jarre Island. The goods were sealed in the infirmary's warehouses along with the porters.

The city's officials were confused by the conflict between the surgeon's diagnosis and his actions. They ordered two more surgeons to the infirmary. They examined the afflicted and found that three porters were already showing buboes. On 8 July 1720, the surgeon-major Coizec and master surgeon Bouzon certified to the city that plague was indeed present. Their official report stated that porters had fallen ill after opening bales of cotton. They noted buboes the size of hen's eggs on the porters' groins. In addition, one of the porters had a suppurating pustule on the thigh. Every patient presented similar symptoms: weak pulse, slight fever, sunken eyes, dry tongue and constant headaches. The report recommended a severe solution. The goods were to be removed to Jarre Island and there, with the ships, burned. Unfortunately, this tardy reaction was further undermined by the quarantine. Instead of a full quarantine, the passengers who had been shipped to Jarre Island were only required to fulfil the 'ordinary' quarantine of fifteen to twenty days. This was the quarantine used at the infirmary for arrivals assumed to be healthy. Since they had originally been admitted to the infirmary, it would appear that their quarantines were not altered to reflect the changed circumstances. Whatever the reason, passengers (along with their clothes and some personal items) were allowed to leave the island for the city. They were lightly fumigated, but no other precautions were taken. In addition, the news that plague had been certified became widely known. The city government had been trying to keep the information secret to prevent flight (which now occurred) and a disruption of trade. Once the news became common knowledge, the city's officials were forced to notify the provincial and national authorities, who took steps to quarantine the city and its rural hinterland.

Despite the official notification that plague was present, the infirmary's surgeon continued to deny the diagnosis. However, it became increasingly impossible to keep the danger of the situation a secret. While he had been endeavouring to deny the presence of plague, other physicians and surgeons working within the city were reporting cases of illness. Women, men and youths were examined for signs of the pestilence in the Rue de Belle Table, the Place de Linche and the Rue de l'Escale. On 9 July, a day after the official finding of plague in the infirmary, two doctors – Mon. Peysonnel and his son – unequivocally diagnosed plague in the Place de Linche. All the suspected cases had been transported at night to the infirmary to avoid public panic; and, in the infirmary, they had all subsequently died. The following day saw the death of a Mon. Boyal, who had been a passenger on Captain Chataud's ship. He had been released after the ordinary (shorter) quarantine. He died that same day and was discovered to have had a bubo under his arm. Porters who were confined at the infirmary were sent under cover of darkness to collect the body and bury it at the infirmary. Throughout these early days and weeks of the epidemic, a clear pattern in official and bureaucratic behaviour is seen to be emerging. The state was doing everything it could either to avoid admitting that plague was present or, failing that, to keep anyone from realising the extent of the danger. At all cost, the officials wanted to prevent a general quarantine of the city, since they knew that that would have a devastating effect on trade. In addition, once the people understood the situation, mass flight would occur with all its attendant disruptive consequences.

Because of official reticence and the attitude of the infirmary's surgeon, the people were lulled into believing that whatever disease was present, it was not a serious epidemic. Isolated plague deaths were not unknown and some had even occurred the year before. In other words, the mere presence of plague was not enough to panic a population. People had to become convinced that the pestilence had indeed taken hold. In effect, the citizenry would panic when they thought the locality was infected. For the most part, individuals were as keen as officials to believe that a general outbreak was unlikely. No one wanted to face the prospect of mass mortality or the collapse of trade and order. 'But', as Bertrand wrote, 'the subtle destroyer, mocking alike the precautions of the wise and the jokes of the incredulous, was secretly insinuating itself far and wide'. More suspicious deaths were reported and investigated in the Place des Prescheurs and the Rue de l'Oratoire. Mon. Sicard, the physician at the Misericorde Hospital certified a plague death on 18 July, but the next day, Mon. Bouzon, a master-surgeon, re-examined the corpse at the request of the city's officials and diagnosed a 'worm fever'. Sicard was so angry at having his professional diagnosis questioned that, although he continued his work, he refused to make any more reports to the state 'to avoid exposing himself to the same slight as he had before received'. Thus, any speedy reaction to the impending crisis was hampered both by official self-deception and by professional in-fighting.

On 23 July, fourteen people were found dead in the same street. Peysonnel (physician) and Bouzon (master-surgeon) examined the bodies. Bouzon diagnosed a common fever, while Peysonnel again certified plague. The consistent unwillingness of some surgeons to accept the presence of plague mystified Bertrand. The indecision amongst the medical professionals and bureaucratic officials was a source of annoyance to both provincial and royal authorities. Bertrand considered the reliance on, and credence of, the surgeons by the city's leaders not only as a personal and professional slight, but also as a ludicrous acceptance of inferior learning and training 'in a city where there was a college and a corporate body of physicians'. By the end of July, the sheer scale of the problem was forcing the hand of the state. Although victims had been successfully moved at night 'to avoid alarming the people', the infirmary was becoming swamped by the number of cases. The officials turned to the College of Physicians to appoint an attending (resident) physician for the infirmary. The college turned to Mon. Michel, who had the least seniority and was 'unembarrassed by a family', to take up the dangerous post. Worse for the politicians and bureaucrats, the younger Peysonnel took over the work of his aged father and refused to keep the scale of the epidemic secret. Not only did he discuss the pestilence with all and sundry in the city, but he also sent letters to various neighbouring towns and villages to alert them of the danger of contact with Marseilles.

Once the outbreak became public knowledge, officialdom at its diverse levels was forced to take appropriate and immediate action. The *parlement* (the supreme judicial – not legislative – body) of Provence forbade contact with the city and its inhabitants under pain of death. Furthermore, the city now selected a committee of trained personnel to deal with the outbreak. Each quarter of the city was to be assigned a doctor (from the team of Bertrand, Raymond, Audon and Robert), a master-surgeon, an assistant surgeon and an apothecary. Immediately, this panel agreed that plague was present and it was the worst outbreak they had ever seen. Within a week, the newly-exposed epidemic had grown to such an extent that the infirmary was full and the sick had to be confined in their homes. Despite having been forced to act, the magistrates still implied that their medical personnel were being alarmist and accused them of making a 'Mississippi' (presumably a big, murky, sluggish flood) of the situation. This public attack on the medical men led to individuals insulting them in the street and accusing them of overstating the crisis for financial gain.

It seems impossible to believe that so many people were unwilling to accept the presence of pestilence. However, there were some good reasons for this incredulity. First, Michel (at the infirmary) continued to diagnose the disease as a common malady (exacerbated by ennui). What was needed, he said, was less panic and more mercury, which may imply that the dispute among the medical personnel had its roots in the ongoing 'turf wars' between chemical and non-chemical medics. Michel was especially keen to point out that although his patients all died within three days, most voided worms from every orifice soon after death. This, he asserted (and many concurred), was a sign of a putrefying fever caused by spoiled or overripe fruit. Finally, in the early weeks of the epidemic, most of the victims were poor and, especially, children. Since everyone was aware that plague was no respecter of persons, many inferred that the cause might not be pestilence. However, as Bertrand cautioned, 'wait but a moment, and a frightful carnage shall force conviction upon you'. Even officially-ordered autopsies failed to settle the dispute – in any case, as Bertrand noted, the dissecting surgeon, Guion, died within days.

While controversy raged within Marseilles and threatened the populace with the unhindered spread of pestilence, the provincial authorities were slowed by no such uncertainty. By mid-August, the quarantine of the city had so limited the flow of grain that the city's bakers failed to produce the requisite number of loaves for the people. With the danger of some unspecified disease now compounded by the very well-defined threat of famine, the people took to the streets in bread riots. Marseilles' governor, the Marquis de Pillas, suggested that markets could be set outside the city. Farmers and merchants could bring produce that would then be left while citizens were restrained behind barriers. Then the bakers and others would be given access to the merchandise. The *parlement* agreed to discuss the matter and asked that Marseilles send a delegation of officials and physicians to meet with a provincial committee to discuss details of the plan. However, when the Marquis de Vauvenargues arrived for the meeting at Notre-Dame-de-la-Doùanne, the Marseilles delegation was comprised only of Mon. Estelle (first *échevin* – or magistrate – of the city) and the city secretary. Bertrand claimed that the city council was still determined to keep the actual scale of the epidemic a secret. Despite the city's obfuscation, the meeting agreed to establish two grain markets, on the roads to Toulon and Aix, and a seafood market at the coastal village of Estaque. This solution removed the immediate threat of famine, but many products simply disappeared from the local diet. The wine merchants had fled and meat proved impossible to import through the convoluted process imposed on the extramural markets. In addition, wages and prices rose because of the dearth and the flight of some workers. Finally, the garrison commander insisted that his troops be supplied with their full ration, regardless of the consequences for the general populace. Thus, Marseilles' citizens were left with the most meagre of provisions.

There was, of course, more to the desire to deny the presence of plague than a need to avoid the collapse of social order and trade. The reality was, as Bertrand confessed, that most people (even medics) realised that 'in the majority of instances, [plague] eludes all the skill of the physicians and the force of medicine'. The real threat of plague from the point of view of the officials was psychological – that people would give way to despair and its corollary, Epicureanism. Indeed, most medical treatments were more likely to harm the patient, or even hasten death, than cure him. For example, Bertrand noted that the surgeon of the galleys (the contingent of the royal Mediterranean fleet stationed in Marseilles), Mon. Audibert, preferred a three-stage treatment. First, he applied strong emetics (to induce vomiting), which he called his 'ferrets'. Then he dosed his patients with copious quantities of tea and other diuretic drinks. Finally, he applied strong purgatives (or laxatives). In the end, his patients were so weakened and dehydrated that most died. After four centuries of pestilence, most would have agreed with Bertrand that 'the establishment of good order, and a wise [set of regulations], are the most certain means of preventing the progress of the contagion' – and clearly better than direct medical intervention.

The preservation of the galley fleet was one of the problems facing the officials and was of national importance. The constant threat of North African corsairs and the Spanish meant it was crucial that the operational abilities of the fleet remain unimpaired. The navy's officers immediately quarantined the entire fleet from the city. They established three separate medical facilities. The first was between the galleys and the quayside. Here, in temporary tents, patients were assessed. Those that showed clear signs of plague were dispatched to the second facility for victims of the pestilence. Others, when a clear diagnosis could be made, were sent to the third hospital for non-plague patients. Thus, a triage centre was used to segregate plague sufferers from others in ill health. The fleet's medical team arranged for eight visits a day to the triage hospital, so plague victims could be identified and segregated as quickly as possible. This quick and disciplined response seems to lend support to Bertrand's enthusiasm for 'good order'.

Although the galleys were extremely confined and oared wholly by convicts, the aggressive quarantine imposed by the fleet's officers greatly lessened the impact of the epidemic. The disease followed the same seasonal pattern in its attack, but was unable to infect (or kill) as many. Thus, August (170 dead), September (286) and October (179) were the worst months, with a sharp decline thereafter in November (89), December (38) and the first two months of 1721 (15 dead). No deaths were reported in March 1721. The toll was particularly high among medical personnel, though, with four surgeons, one apothecary and six almoners dying. However, the overall impact was much less severe. Of the 10,000 personnel in the galleys and arsenal, only about 1,300 fell ill (13 per cent) and a paltry 800 actually died (8 per cent). The mortality rate among those inflicted (62 per cent) shows that the disease, when it was able to penetrate the fleet's defences, while less virulent than in the city (where 83 per cent of the infected died), was still not exactly mild. The fundamental difference would appear to have been the prompt action of the officers in confining anyone displaying any symptoms of illness and then segregating those with lesser diseases from the plague victims. This probably prevented the infection of the sailors already weakened with some other ailment. In addition, it appears that the quarantining measures managed to limit the infection rate of the group (13 per cent in the fleet compared with nearly 70 per cent in the city).

Bertrand lays the blame for the large number of infections and subsequent deaths in the city squarely on the shoulders of the city's ruling officials and, to a lesser extent, some of his fellow medical practitioners. The refusal of the *échevins* to appoint a separate health committee because it would dilute their power was especially criticised. Indeed, the city's leaders even refused to permit a doctor to attend their meetings. In response (and a fit of pique), the physicians simply passed them a copy of Ranchin's *Treatise on the Plague* as an alternative guide. Sicard, the doctor of the Misericorde Hospital, who had been offended when his diagnosis was questioned, did manage to convince the city of the possible efficacy of city-wide fumigation. As in London, the decision was taken to light fires. However, the Marseilles approach was considerably more comprehensive than in London. It was decreed that on three consecutive evenings from five o'clock onwards, huge fires were to be lit in the main plazas and thoroughfares. In addition, small fires were ordered before each private house and sulphur was to be burned in every room. All cloth was to be draped in the open and thereby cleansed. Bertrand, who consistently ridiculed the miasmic view of the disease, said this action was simply a waste of valuable winter fuel. Moreover, he turned the miasmic theory against its advocates, arguing that creating great clouds of smoke (a smog inversion) would simply trap the bad air in the city, rather than it being blown out to sea by the prevailing (health-bringing) winds which normally blessed Marseilles.

As August progressed, it soon became clear throughout Marseilles that the plague had a firm grip on the city and the situation was only going to worsen. Unsurprisingly, many began to flee. Unfortunately for them, the provincial *cordon sanitaire* was extremely effective. Trapped between the armed guards on the quarantine barriers and the plague-ridden streets of Marseilles, many simply moved into tents in the fields immediately outside the walls. Others took to the caves in the hills above Marseilles and the more adventurous moved themselves on to boats in the harbour. Because of the effective and speedy actions of the provincial and royal officials, the only people who had been able to flee were the 10,000 who had got out at the first hint of danger. One would be unlikely to experience a shock upon learning that most officials (who had hidden or denied the plague's presence in the early weeks of the outbreak) had managed to escape. Unlike London, the clergy remained, though nuns were dispersed from their convents to their family homes. The *échevins* now instituted crisis legislation. All indigents were to be removed from the streets. Officials were selected to ensure that every poor person received a set bread ration each day. Vagabonds, indigents and poor strangers were conscripted to collect and bury the corpses accumulating in the streets. Mass graves were dug. Finally, shops were closed, church services cancelled and the courts suspended. It was soon apparent that there was insufficient burial space. The infirmary's courtyard was filled and the bishop refused to allow the cathedral grounds to be used. Eventually, two large pits were opened outside the walls, but with 300-400 corpses per day, these filled quickly.

Moreover, the physicians continued to complain that not enough was being done for the living. In particular, they clamoured against home quarantine. They felt that locking the healthy in a house with their infected relatives would only increase the death toll. Instead, they suggested that the city take over the poorhouse (Hôtel de la Charité), which was separated slightly from the rest of the city. It had space for 600 people and, more importantly, touched no less than six religious houses (giving room for expansion should the crisis deepen). The physicians reckoned that, at a pinch, the whole complex could safely and conveniently hold over 3,000 afflicted people. However, this innovative plan was rejected by those in charge of the hostel. Even when the city concurred, nothing was done to implement the proposal. Instead, the Hôtel Dieu, a smaller structure, was requisitioned. It filled up in two days. Never at ease with the college, the *échevins* also imported two physicians (Guyon, father and son) from Barjolx. Bertrand said that their short stay only worsened things, since they used extreme applications of bloodletting and purgatives. Soon after their arrival, the father died and the son tried to flee. Falling ill in a cabin outside the walls, his body was burnt along with the structure. The rest of the medical staff at the Hôtel Dieu died and the situation degenerated into chaos. As a result, from 20 August to 1 October, the city had no functioning plague hospital and the infected were simply placed in tents which lined the outside of the walls.

❖     ❖     ❖

One of the most complex aspects of the Marseilles plague remains the complicated and antagonistic relationship between the officials and the medical practitioners, and even amongst the medical people themselves. On 12 August, in an effort to circumvent their local medical advisors and to quell the rising panic, the *échevins* received a delegation of learned doctors sent by the Crown from the great medical university at Montpellier. They were asked to examine the situation and to report to the officials. The meeting at which the report was presented was held in secret and no local medical men were present. The *échevins* reported to the city that the visiting physicians had decided that the epidemic was a malignant (non-contagious) fever caused by bad food. In fact, this was a complete fabrication, as the physicians made clear to the Crown. They had reported unanimously that plague was present and likely to worsen. The statements issued by the *échevins* were a studied attempt to limit the panic and to avoid an even tighter provincial quarantine.

However, Bertrand did report that, as the pestilence worsened, the problems within the medical community lessened. More importantly, he had high praise for the fortitude of his fellow practitioners (of every variety) in the face of the crisis. The twelve physicians in the college were assigned various areas to cover: two went to the arsenal, two to the hospital for the sailors, one each to the infirmary, the Hôtel Dieu, the Abbey St-Victeur, and four to visit the sick in their homes. Only one fled the city and he was already in very poor health. Of the various surgeons (masters, residents, and apprentices), only six fled Marseilles. The numerous apothecaries were especially praiseworthy, with only one defection from their ranks. Thus, the city was well provided with medical workers, but the ineffective actions taken by the officials continued to hamper and, indeed, thwart, efforts to halt the progress of the pestilence. 'Rich and poor, male and female, young and old, alike became its victims, and the whole town was filled with mourning and tears'. By late August, the mortality was at its height and had even been worsened by the effects of the quarantine: 'the misery and dearth [was] almost as general as the contagion'. As Pepys had observed in London, despair and fear meant that 'all charity was extinguished in every breast'.

As already noted, the city was spared the terror of facing the disease without benefit of clergy. Although the Anglican ministers had, for the most part, fled London, the Catholic priests and monks stayed. Bertrand singled out the cathedral canons, though for a special rebuke. Only one of them remained. However, most parish priests stayed at their posts and the monks were especially assiduous in their labours, with dire consequences. For example, of the thirty-one Jesuits, twenty-nine were infected and twenty died. The bishop's efforts earned him heroic status in the minds and hearts of the people. He moved freely about the city with total disregard for his own welfare. In mid-September he ordered that those clerics who had fled must return under pain of being deprived of their benefices. In one case, he allowed the monks of an entire monastery to be stripped of their benefices and replaced by others when they were tardy in returning.

The personal tragedies were, of course, the worst aspect of the plague. However, the cumulative impact of the disease simply made the situation even more heart-rending. The afflicted quickly abandoned their houses to seek comfort in the city's major boulevards and promenades. Struggling with fevers, they wanted access to water and fresh breezes. However, lying in the street, Bertrand admitted that they were avoided by all Christians and the only hope they had for small acts of charity was from Turks or other Muslims. The dead and dying, who sought shelter under its trees, almost wholly covered the Rue Dauphine (300 metres long and 10 metres wide) that ran towards the hospital. The piles of corpses were so high that the weight crushed and burst those on the bottom adding to the stench and danger – and horror – of the pestilence. The hospital that housed the city's poor and orphaned children was a scene of utter loss. Of the 2,000-3,000 children there, only 100 survived; the rest died behind its doors. In February 1721, the steward was hanged for his mismanagement of the crisis. At one point, in an effort to die on holy ground, the afflicted dragged themselves to the cathedral, where over 1,000 corpses eventually accumulated. If human corpses were not enough, the people slaughtered dogs and threw them into the sea, which promptly tossed their bodies up on to the quays and promenades of the city.

Confronted by the mounting disaster (and corpses), the city's officials finally acted. They accepted the offer of help from the fleet's officers, who promised 133 convicts their freedom if they would help clear the bodies from the streets. Overall, five tasks confronted the *échevins*. Firstly, they needed to restore order. Then they were to provide food, recall officials and punish looters. Finally, Marseilles' leaders had to find some way to control prices to ensure an adequate (and affordable) supply of food. By late August, the mortality rate had reached nearly 1,000 dead per day. The city considered various emergency measures for dealing with the bodies. Cremation was rejected because it was feared that the smoke would only spread the plague. Someone suggested that the bodies be placed in ships and sunk at sea, but it was feared that the bodies would simply float to the surface in a few days and then be thrown on to the shore along with the dogs' bodies. Burying the bodies beneath the streets was not feasible, nor was the idea that they be piled in heaps and heavily limed. Eventually, the city decided to stuff them into the vaults beneath the city's churches with large quantities of lime in an effort to dissolve them quickly. The 1,000 bodies on the seaside at La Tourette promenade were dumped into a hole in an old city wall and buried under rubble. Although these methods began to lessen the quantity of bodies in the street, it was clear that they could not keep pace with the growing problem.

Eventually, the obvious incompetence of the *échevins* led the Regent (Phillippe, Duc d'Orleans, 1674-1723), on behalf of Louis XV (1710-1774), to appoint De Langeron as temporary commander of the city. He decided that three matters were of the highest priority: restore order, provide hospital spaces for the afflicted and dig more grave pits. On 12 September, De Langeron began his work. He ordered the recall of all notaries (necessary for wills to be made), midwives (too many women and children were dying in childbirth) and officials under severe penalties for disobedience. He ordered the removal of all clothes, furniture and waste from the streets. In addition, the fishermen were told to net the dogs' bodies and drag them out to sea. He also recruited a large number of medical workers to replenish the now depleted ranks of local practitioners – over a dozen physicians and master-surgeons were hired. However, the cost of enticing someone to work in so dangerous a setting was both high and an opportunity for extortion. Mon. Pons, a physician from Languedoc, demanded £6,000 per month while in the city and a further £1,000 annual pension thereafter for himself, his wife and children. The city had no choice but to agree. De Langeron, much to the disgust of Bertrand, even admitted Mon. Varin, his wife and nephew who were 'empirics' (chemical physicians) with their 'specific' (chemical curative or elixir), which they sold for £20 per bottle. The financial burden was somewhat eased, as it had been in London, by the generous donations that poured in from the rest of the country – a Mon. Laun alone gifted £100,000 to Marseilles.

As the efforts of De Langeron began to take hold, the situation improved. The removal of the bodies was a great boon, allowing shops to reopen and some sense of normality to return. Also, civic leaders who had fled began slowly to resume their responsibilities. Finally, on 3 October, royal troops arrived to secure the city's gates. The following day, a plague hospital was finally opened at La Charité and the nearby Jeu-de-Mail building. The physicians Robert and Bouthillier were placed in charge of the former and Pons and Guilhermin of the latter. Guilhermin died soon thereafter and was replaced by Audon. The medical personnel were better organised, too, with Chycoineau given command of physicians and the surgeons placed under the control of Soulliers and Nellaton. At long last, the city had sufficient beds for the afflicted, just as the total number of infected began to decline. Although the drop in new cases was most welcome, Bertrand noted that the mortality rate was as high as ever. Nevertheless, it was obvious to everyone that the pestilence was not only lessening, but also that the city was finally coping with the situation.

Bertrand noted that the improving situation had the effect of encouraging people to venture forth. Although feeling somewhat braver, the wariness of individuals was apparent in their behaviour. They carried 8-10ft-long poles (so-called *bâtons de St Roch*) to maintain a 'safe' distance between themselves and anyone else. However, just as things looked better, the disease finally struck the wealthiest quarter of the city (St Ferreol) with a vengeance. The return of the rich as a result of the restoration of order may be to blame in part. As Bertrand commented, the rich had fled and now returned. Thus, '[the rich] are always the last attacked by a contagion, on account of the means they have to place themselves out of its reach'. Nothing could protect the afflicted from the disastrous efforts of the imported doctors who, Bertrand said, killed as effectively and as efficiently as the pestilence. They prescribed repeated bleedings, violent emetics, strong laxatives and lanced the buboes (causing severe shock).

❖         ❖         ❖

The last week of October brought universal relief to the city when no new cases were reported. Although a few cases appeared in early November, it was clear that the pestilence was waning. On 15 November, the bishop went to the top of the tower of the parish church at Accoulles and sounded the bells, while the galleys fired their cannons. These signals were meant to call people to prayer,

*A barber-surgeon bleeding a woman in the late seventeenth century.*

either at home or before the churches, for deliverance and thanks-giving. The people of Marseilles, and their rulers, now faced the daunting task of coping with the aftermath of the plague. Body collection was speeded up as nearly 700 convicts were drafted in. Their efforts quickly cleared the streets of the corpses. A more bizarre effect of the lessening of the disease was a rush to marry. Bertrand noted that the poor now found themselves richer and therefore able to afford better dowries. In addition, sons and daughters were either freed from parental control (their parents being dead) or no longer blocked by elder children and thus able to marry. Widows, widowers and many others rushed from gravesides to altars. To prevent this behaviour from re-igniting the plague, the city insisted that prospective newlyweds have health certificates. More obviously, the city also had to cope with a massive caseload of criminal prosecutions arising from the closure of the courts in the summer and the substantial increase in theft, looting and riotous living which the plague had occasioned.

There were other consequences to the plague. Some of the physicians decided to publish tracts repudiating, as they saw it, four popular errors about the pestilence that had been apparent in the popular reaction. First, they denied that the plague was the result of Divine wrath and concluded instead that it was a natural event. One might assume from this view that modernity, in the form of early Enlightenment thought, had begun to have a profound effect on medical thought. However, when one turns in their tracts from theology to medicine, one realises that little had really changed since the first outbreaks in the 1340s. They denied that plague was an incurable malady, though they were unable to offer any certain cure. Next, they scoffed at any suggestion that the disease was contagious rather than purely miasmic. Finally, they rejected the popular view that fire (fumigation) and flight were the only effective responses to pestilence. In effect, while they criticised the traditional interpretations of theologians, they were still clinging to the unchanging verities of their own profession.

On a more practical level, the officials had to begin the difficult task of purifying the city. Every house that had been infected was marked with a red cross. All the (cloth) contents of these houses were to be put into the street. Anything from these piles that was not worth salvaging was to be burned in the public squares. Then the houses, along with the furnishings, were to be fumigated with aromatic herbs and gunpowder. After the fumigation, the walls, floors and ceilings were to be scrubbed thoroughly and washed two or three times with a lime wash. Everything put into the street that could be salvaged was to be labelled and taken outside the walls for boil-washing by people who had recovered (that is, been made temporarily immune) from plague. Those who could pay for these costly activities were expected to recompense the state. Once a house and its contents were completely purified, a white cross was painted over the red one. The quantity of material needing cleansing was enormous, since many merchants made 'a sort of warehouse of the vestibule of their homes'. Since a rumour circulated that all cloth would be burned, initially many people hid their belongings.

The churches were in an even worse state since their vaults were packed with corpses. The buildings were to be cleansed as well, but sacred objects were only to be fumigated by the priests. After a lengthy meeting of civic officials, physicians, surgeons, architects and masons, the bishop was forced to intervene with the only possible solution to the problem of the vaults. He ordered that they be bricked up and sealed with iron bars and thick cement. All other suggestions about flooding them with lime, vinegar or fumigants were deemed hopelessly inadequate for the task. Despite the loss of privileges suffered by the clergy and the wealthy in being deprived of their burial spaces, the bishop decreed that the vaults would remain sealed for the foreseeable future. To avoid any possible re-infection, even after the churches were cleansed, the lay people were kept out of them. Services during Holy Week in 1721 were held behind closed doors, while the parishioners waited outside.

# A
# SCHEME
### FOR
## Proper Methods to be taken, ſhould it pleaſe G O D to viſit us with the
# PLAGUE.

*By Sir* JOHN COLBATCH, *A Member of the* College of Phyſicians.

## LONDON:
Printed by J. DARBY, and ſold by J. RO-BERTS in *Warwick-Lane*, and A. DODD without *Temple-Bar.* M. DCC. XXI.

[ Price 4 *d.* ]

*The Marseilles outbreak caused concern in Britain and writers looked back to accounts of the London plague of 1665. This publication was typical of the time dispensing advice on measures that should be taken in dealing with plague.*

However, at Easter the crowds forced their way into the churches and thereafter Mass returned to normal.

Finally, Bertrand was quick to note that the mortality had a greater impact than the mere numbers would suggest. He noted that many trade groups were devastated by the pestilence. Of 100 master-hatters, fifty-three died. Of the 300 journeyman hatters, only about 10 per cent survived. The 104 master-joiners lost 81 per cent of their members. The shoemakers saw 110 (55 per cent) of their 200 members die. The master tailors lost 57 per cent. An astonishing 93 per cent of the cobblers died, while the masons lost no less than 70 per cent of their membership. As has been noted in previous chapters, the dead could perhaps be replaced by immigration and birth, but the loss of skilled workers had a long-term and profound impact on any community. Marseilles was no exception.

❖          ❖          ❖

In the first half-century of the plague in Western Europe, the best estimates are that the population declined by at least 50 per cent. As if to remind Europeans of its potency, the last attack of the pestilence deprived one of Europe's leading trading centres of the same percentage in less than twelve months. Marseilles serves as the most vivid reminder of the devastating power of the plague and the hopeless impotence of man in combating it. Greed, stupidity, incompetence and myth all conspired to help the plague gain a stranglehold on the city in 1720, but it was the disease itself that killed over 80 per cent of those it infected. While most readers will be more familiar with the great plague of London – for reasons of literature, history and language – the reality is that the Marseilles plague was more dramatic. Not only was it the last outbreak in Western Europe, but it was also one of the most devastating plagues ever to strike a major city.

# DEATH'S MANY FACES
## Other 'Plagues'

*Concerning the plagues that we see among [the Indians] I cannot help but feel that God is telling us: 'You are hastening to exterminate this race. I shall help you to wipe them out more quickly [with smallpox]'.*

A Catholic friar in New Spain

ne of the most important aspects of the history of plague is that it was but one of many epidemic diseases to ravage various communities in the medieval and early modern periods. Its continuing grip on the popular imagination and memory has little relationship with its actual history. Other diseases such as influenza, smallpox, and measles probably killed as many people. Syphilis, tuberculosis and leprosy debilitated and killed significant numbers of individuals as well. Famine and war, typhoid/typhus, yellow fever and cholera also took an enormous toll. What then made – and makes – plague stand out. First, the sudden onslaught of the Black Death in the fourteenth century left a permanent scar on the psyche of Western Europeans. Secondly, unlike many of Europe's other diseases that carried off large numbers of children, the elderly and the infirm, plague killed otherwise healthy people in the prime of their life. This ability to strike the key members of a community helps explain its profound impact on demography and the economy. Finally, most of the other diseases were a regular feature of life. That is, people died of them on an annual basis.

In real terms, smallpox might have killed as many but it did so a few at a time and mostly struck the young. Plague left a community untouched for up to two decades only to reappear, killing a quarter to one half of the population in a few months. The very haphazard unpredictability of plague made it even more frightening and the ferocity of any given attack made plague stand out in the memory (and, hence, history) of a society. Most people died of a bacterial or viral disease or perhaps of crises such as war and famine in the medieval or early modern world; few died of old age after the failure of major organ systems. So, disease was not a surprise. Epidemics were not unexpected. Plague stood out in the memory and experience of the people it afflicted, and continues to stand out in the minds of their descendants, because of its unpredictability and ferocity. Plague did not just kill people; it destroyed communities. Plague was not a regular and unremitting danger faced by every one every day; it was an irregular disaster. Plague was not just an unpleasant accompaniment to a difficult life; it was the very personification of Death.

❖     ❖     ❖

The disease that evidenced the greatest similarity of reactions to plague at the popular, elite and professional level was leprosy. Indeed, the *lazaretto* of plague outbreaks mentioned so often above was in fact a development of leper houses (*leprosaria*). In many cases, former leper houses were converted into a city's lazaretto until a purpose-built hospital could be constructed. Moreover, attitudes to lepers and leprosy were very similar to, and actually conditioned, those of people to plague victims and the epidemic itself. Indeed, it is the understanding of leprosy as a mark of divine disfavour and wrath that was so easily adapted to understanding and explaining plague outbreaks that is of the most interest.

IL SVCCESSO
DELLA PESTE
OCCORSA IN
PADOVA
L'ANNO M.D.LXXVI.

Scritta, & veduta per Alef-
fandro Canobbio.

CON PRIVILEGIO.

IN VENETIA,
Appreſſo Gratioſo Perchacino.
M.D.LXXVII.

DE PESTE
QVAESTIO-
NES DVAE EXPLI-
CATÆ: VNA, SITNE
CONTAGIOSA: ALTE-
ra, an & quatenus ſit Chriſtianis per
ſeceſſionem vitanda.

Theodoro Beza Vezelio
auctore.

GENEVÆ,
Apud Euſtathium Vignon.
cIɔ Iɔ LXXIX.

These four title pages of accounts of plague, ranging from the sixteenth to the
eighteenth century, demonstrate the special concern evinced by the plague and the
keenness with which information was sought by the authorities.

RELAZIONE
ISTORICA
DELLA PESTE,
CHE ATTACCOSSI
A MESSINA
Nell'anno mille ſettecento
quarantatre.
COLL' AGGIVNTA
DEGLI ORDINI, EDITTI, ISTRUZIONI,
E altri atti pubblici fatti in occaſione
della medeſima.

IN PALERMO Appreſſo Angelo Felicella MDCCXLV.
CON LICENZA DE' SVPERIORI, E PRIVILEGIO.

A ſpeſe di Pietro Bentivegna Librajo.

RELATIONI
DI VARIE PESTI
in Italia ſin'all'anno corrente 1630.
Con tutti li ſegni di quelle, e rimedij eſperimentati
nella vera cura, e preſerua.
Con il modo di purgar le robbe, e caſe infette,
mandate da varij Medici aſiſtenti
in detta cura.
Stampate per ordine del Magiſtrato della Sanità in Venetia,
e riſtampate in Napoli, ad inſtanza d'Andrea Paladino.

IN NAPOLI,
Appreſſo Ottauio Beltrano M.DC.XXXI
Con licenza de' Superiori.
Si vendeno nella Libraria d'Andrea Paladino.

Leprosy was understood to be a punishment sent by God on certain individuals (rather than communities) for hidden sins (or even thoughts). Specifically, lepers were thought to have been secretly guilty of especially revolting and disgusting sins of a sexual nature. However, there is considerable debate suggesting that leprosy (Hansen's disease) may not actually have existed in Western Europe prior to the Black Death. As a biological disease, literary evidence (other than the Bible) dates the disease as far back as 600 BC in India. Pagan sources from the Greco-Roman world, Orthodox Byzantine authors and later Islamic medical writers treated the disease purely as a physical affliction that produced gross disfigurement (and, ultimately, death). However, in the West, leprosy became conflated with heresy by the seventh century. A leper was a person with incorrect beliefs and practices, which were given visible form (by God) under the guise of a skin ailment.

The confusion of leprosy, the disease, with leprosy, a spiritual condition, arose from confusion in translating Hebrew accounts of the disease in the Bible into Greek and, later, Latin. In the Law of the Hebrew Bible, lepers were individuals who were people (or things or even homes) marked by some obvious blemishes of a mouldy or scaly nature. These people and objects would then be examined by priests and declared 'leprous' or not. Once a diagnosis was made certifying the disease the infected person or object was separated from God's people (or their use) until the priests could ensure that the 'blemish' had been removed. The Hebrew word used was *zara'at* (or 'ritual impurity'). In other words, leprosy in the Biblical law refers to a quality of purity rather than a specific disease. Indeed, many scholars state unequivocally that Hansen's disease was not even present in Biblical times.

When the Bible was translated into Greek (in the Septuagint) for Hellenised Jews more familiar with Greek than Hebrew, the word *lepra* was used. This referred to leprosy as well as conditions such as mould and scaliness. The Greek word denoted a relatively undefined form of blemish rather than a specific clinical condition. When Constantinus Africanus (*c.*1020-87) translated Islamic medical texts on the physical condition, instead of transliterating the Arabic (*judhäm*), he translated it into the Greek as *lepra*, the more general word. Latin sources then used *lepra*. Thus, a single word became used in Western sources for other literary references to a moral blemish (*zara'at*) and a degenerative disease (*judhäm*, Hansen's disease). In effect, this meant that anyone presenting with any skin blemish might be suspected of leprosy and, hence, of secret and gross immorality. Moreover, any person separately suspected of some hidden evil would be expected to have some blemish on their person. Most importantly of all, in the period with the highest incidence of 'leprosy' (*c.*1090-1363), which has been referred to as the 'Great Leper Hunt' (an allusion to the later witch hunts), diagnosis was, as in the Bible, the responsibility of the priests. However, by the time of the Black Death, medical doctors became involved in the diagnosis of leprosy. Under the direction of treatises – for example, Guy de Chauliac (*c.*1300-68), *La Grande Chirurgie*, 1363 – that clearly defined the disease (Hansen's) by symptoms, fewer and fewer 'lepers' were being identified.

This raises the interesting possibility that leprosy in the three centuries before the Black Death was not actually a disease but a socially constructed category of individual – a state of mind, an artificially constructed social category. People did not get leprosy, they were lepers. As Hansen's disease is (and appears always to have been) actually very rare, some such interpretation is necessary to understand the extremely high incidence of the disease in the eleventh to the fourteenth centuries. Several thousand *leprosaria* were constructed throughout Western Europe in this period. If one assumes the conservative figure of fourteen lepers per house, the 220 *leprosaria* in England and Scotland provided accommodation for 3,080 lepers (servicing a population of only 1.5 million).

When one examines views expressed about leprosy, it becomes clear that something other than a specific disease is being discussed. St Louis IX (1215-70) of France, the great Crusader and religious zealot, said that 'you ought to know that there is no lep-rosy as ugly as the leprosy of being in mortal sin, because the soul that is in mortal sin is like the devil'. In the mid-twelfth century, a Parisian monastic chronicler wrote that 'fornicators, concubines, the incestuous, adulterers, the avaricious, usurers, false witnesses, perjurers ... all, I say, such as these, who through guilt are cut off from God, all are judged to be leprous by the priests'. In *Cor nostrum*, a bull of Pope Alexander III (*c.*1105-1181), King Baldwin IV (*c.*1161-85) of Jerusalem was declared a leper because he did not feel anything when stuck with pins (that is, his skin was insensitive to pain). Later, witches were said to bear a Devil's Mark which was also insensitive to touch, pain or fire.

While this may explain the stigmatising of certain people as lepers it does not account for the massive increase in leper houses (and inmates). At the Third Lateran Council (1179) under Pope Alexander III, strident attacks were made against sodomy and the Cathar heresy in the south of France. The latter was subsequently destroyed in a bloody and horrific Crusade against heretical Christians (rather than infidels and unbelievers). The Council also attacked lepers. It insisted that they had to be segregated from the community lest they infect others. For this purpose many leper houses were needed and had to be provided with a priest, a chapel and a separate graveyard. The 'quarantine' of lepers was to be complete and permanent. Since there were many more priests than parishes, these houses provided extra employment for clerics. The endowment of leper houses was deemed to be a 'good work' of charity. The Fourth Lateran Council (1215) also required that lepers (and Jews, who were said to be particularly prone to leprosy) were to wear special identifying badges. Lepers were, therefore, a contagion within society, from which society had to be protected. Their danger was less the threat of medical and physical infection than the possibility that their immorality and degeneracy might corrupt others.

Clearly, it is certainly possible that leprosy (Hansen's disease) did actually exist and was simply given a moralising interpretation.

33 A skeleton representing death brandishes an arrow at a young couple. The man raises his arm to protect the woman beside him.

34 In a page from the Placebo, part of the Mass for the Dead, the initial shows a coffin before the altar with three priests chanting the Mass.

35 An illuminated page from an early fifteenth-century Mass for the Dead shows the service taking place.

36 *Above left:* A Dutch manuscript version of the Mass for the Dead. In the initial letter the souls of the departed burn in the flames of purgatory. In the border at the top is an angel carrying a soul while on the right-hand side is a depiction of the harrowing of Hell, a popular medieval image of the defeat of evil by Christ's descent to Hell and the freeing of souls there. At the bottom of the page is a metaphor of this, with a stork feeding her imprisoned young.

37 *Above right:* St Sebastian was a popular saint called on at times of plague. This illustration from a manuscript Book of Hours shows his martyrdom while the Latin text below calls for his intercession. The book belonged to the bastard daughter of the French King Louis XI.

Cōmemora⁹. de ſacto ſebaſtiao
ſanctē ſebaſtiane
ſemp veſpere ȝ mane
horiē cūctie ȝ momēt
ſum adhuc ſum ſane mētis

iſta adeuitandum epidemiā
quātiqȝ et mortem ſubi
tāneam qnam dommis papʒ
cſemoie ſcotue qui ſummue
fuit theologue dicendum deceuᵗ
et conſtrauit euin in conſiſtorio
cum ommibus dommne cardi
naſibue et conceſſit ommibus
audientibue C C pſ. dice in
dulgencie. Omnee veʒo miſſa

38 *Above left:* The martyrdom of St Sebastian, from an early sixteenth-century manuscript connected with la Sainte Chapelle in Paris.

39 *Above right:* The plague saints: St Sebastian, his body pierced with arrows, and St Roch, with his pilgrim's staff and dog – an angel attends to his sore.

40 Burning Jews, in an illustration from the *Nuremberg Chronicle*. Jews were often scapegoated for the spread of the plague and as a result found themselves the victims of pogroms. This picture is taken from the German text of the *Chronicle*.

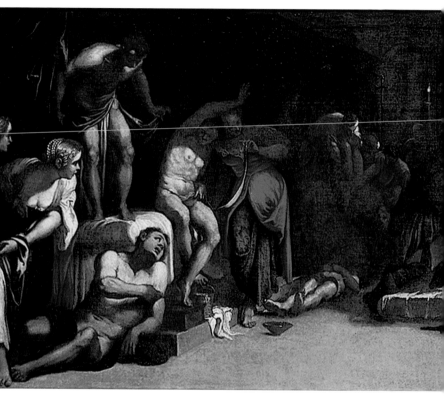

41 The figure of St Roch in a *lazaretto* attending to the sick, after a painting by the Venetian artist Tintoretto.

42 A seventeenth-century depiction of St Carlo Borromeo ministering to plague victims in Milan in 1576. The frequency of flight by both Catholic and Protestant clergy meant that those who did stay, such as Borromeo in Milan or the Bishop of Marseilles in the eighteenth century, became saintly figures.

43 A detail from a seventeenth-century painting showing an angel lancing a bubo on the leg of St Roch. It was assumed that buboes were swollen with the poison of the plague and that lancing them would allow the poison to run out. In fact, the person was more likely to die of shock.

44 Protective clothing worn by physicians dealing with outbreaks of plague:

(i) Beaked costume used during the seventeenth century and at Marseilles in 1720 (*above left*).

(ii) Simple oil-cloth suit, again worn in the seventeenth century and at Marseilles (*above right*).

(iii) The tied cover-all worn by Japanese troops during the 1910 Manchuria outbreak (*left*).

45  A cartoon of Napoleon at Jaffa in 1799, touching the bubo of a plague victim.

46  A British cartoon of Napoleon instructing the doctor to poison the plague victims at Jaffa, George Cruikshank, 1799.

However, numerous excavations of leper cemeteries have failed to produce more than a handful of skeletons showing signs of a disease that should have led to extreme disfigurement. Moreover, true leprosy is normally an ailment that strikes those who are most socially deprived and malnourished. Yet leper houses were not free. With the exception of a few pauper-lepers supported by charitable bequests, the overwhelming majority of inmates in the various *leprosaria* were expected to pay for their 'care'. Lepers, by Papal decree, lost the right to inherit property and could be expelled from the *leprosarium* for bad behaviour. Poor lepers, who could not find a charity bed in an institution, were allowed to beg at church doors and were almost always specifically exempt from anti-begging legislation. All of which seems to imply that the six to twenty lepers per *leprosarium* were confined for spiritual or economic reasons rather than as the result of a specific medical condition.

These same lepers were, therefore, ideal targets for blame in times of crisis. On 21 June 1321, King Philip V (1293-1322) of France declared that all the lepers in France were guilty of high treason since they were conspiring with the Jews, the 'Sultan of Babylon' and the Muslim King of Granada to poison the wells of the kingdom. Lepers and Jews were massacred across France in a harbinger of the destruction of Jews in the late fourteenth and early fifteenth centuries during times of plague. Indeed, as leprosy was seen as a disease that occurred as the direct result of sin, involvement in an act so obviously evil was completely believable. Any gross sinfulness could bring on a leprous blemish and was to be avoided. Arnaud de Vernoilles (Toulouse, 1321) echoed the sentiments, if not the conclusions, of many when he recounted that:

> [while] they were burning the lepers [and the Jews] I had sex with a prostitute. And after I had perpetrated this sin my face began to swell. I was terrified and thought that I had caught leprosy; I thereupon swore that in the future I would never sleep with a woman again; in order to keep this oath, I began to abuse little boys.

By 1338, Pope Benedict XII (d. 1342) was forced to declare that the lepers had been innocent and were the victim of a plot hatched by officials. He said this despite that fact that as Jacques Fournier, Bishop of Pamiers, he had overseen the execution of thousands of lepers in 1321.

Thus, lepers were those people specially marked by God as having merited his wrath for specific sins. An entire system developed for the quarantining of these lepers and the protection of the wider community from their infection and contagion. In times of crisis, these same lepers could be, and were, targeted as scapegoats. Plague presented a different set of problems. By its very nature it was impossible to single out individuals as carriers of contagion. Plague was too indiscriminate and pervasive for so simplistic an interpretation. Thus, it became seen as evidence of communal disease. If leprosy was a moral blemish found on an individual, then plague was a moral blemish found on a community. Nevertheless, the need for confinement, segregation and quarantine remained, as did the inclination to find scapegoats. The plague was a more complex infection on the body politic, but it was dealt with by many of the same measures as those used for leprosy. Most interestingly of all, the appearance of the Black Death coincided with the almost complete disappearance of leprosy. This presented Western European society with thousands of now unused and unwanted buildings designed for the segregation and confinement of contagious people. The coincidental disappearance of leprosy could not have been more convenient.

❖        ❖        ❖

In 1720, on the small north Scottish island of Foula, about 180 people – from a population of 200 – died. This isolated community had been struck by smallpox. As with plague, this disease seems to have been unknown to the ancient world. It was first described, in its mildest form, by the Islamic author Al-Razi in 910. For most of the centuries thereafter, smallpox remained an endemic child-hood disease that struck most young people and killed about five to 10 per cent of those infected. Although many children actually died, for most it was simply an unpleasant ailment that, at its worst, left behind some scarring and, at its best, bequeathed a permanent immunity to those who survived it. However, as with Foula, it was capable of being an extremely virulent and destructive disease if it happened into communities where there had been no contact with the children's variety of the disease.

The virulence of smallpox as an epidemic 'plague' was immedi-ately apparent to the peoples of the New World after 1492. Europeans arrived, carrying the disease into communities with no natural immunity. The Taino people of the Caribbean were almost totally annihilated (the few survivors were exterminated in the work gangs of their Spanish conquerors). The Aztecs, Mayas and Incas saw over a third of their populations destroyed by smallpox within months of the their first contact with Western Europeans. As with plague, the demographic collapse was cumulative and, indeed, exasperated by the harsh rule imposed by the Europeans. In 1518, the Nahuatl-speaking peoples of central Mexico num-bered approximately 25.2 million; by 1605, there were only 1.1 million left – a demographic collapse of nearly 96 per cent. Along the Pacific coast of South America, a population of 6.5 million in 1524 effectively no longer existed in 1590.

The impact of smallpox as an epidemic plague and the immunity of Europeans were completely understood by observers of the day. It was seen as a sign of God's support for European expansion and His displeasure with the pagan and 'barbaric' peoples of the New World. As one (Protestant) Pilgrim wrote, 'the good hand of God favoured our beginning … in sweeping away the great multitudes of Natives by the Small Pox'. John Winthrop (1588-1649), Governor of the Massachusetts Bay Colony, remarked that 'for the natives, they are neere all dead of small Poxe, so as the Lord hathe cleared our title to what we possess'. The (Catholic) Spanish expressed similar views, and a friar in New Spain, wrote that 'concerning the plagues that we see among [the Indians] I cannot help but feel that God is telling us: "You are hastening to extermi-nate this race. I shall help you to wipe them out more quickly"'. What smallpox began, the Europeans were willing to finish. One of the English Colonial soldiers sent against the Pequot of the Connecticut Valley after a severe outbreak of smallpox said of the massacre of the survivors, 'it was a fearful sight to see them thus frying in the fire and the streams of blood quenching the same, and horrible was the stink and scent thereof; but the victory seems a sweet sacrifice [to God]'. So clearly did the invaders understand the importance and effect of epidemic disease that, in 1763, General Sir Jeffrey Amherst (1717-97), Governor-general of British North America, sent infected blankets to the rebellious Indians under the Ottawa chief, Pontiac (c. 1720-69).

In the instance of smallpox, an endemic disease of Western Europe proved to be a plague upon the peoples of the New World equal in scale to the Black Death. Had Europe faced an invasion and migration of outsiders immune to plague in the course of the late fourteenth and early fifteenth centuries, their few remaining descendants might have found themselves confined to a few reser-vations in isolated parts of the Continent. Although never a mass killer of European adults, smallpox remained a dangerous child-hood disease until the eighteenth century. By then, Western Europeans were becoming aware of the inoculation techniques historically employed in parts of Africa and the Islamic world. In 1706, Cotton Mather (1663-1728), the great preacher, learned of this method from a West African slave. He was able to encourage many to begin to inoculate their children by taking some of the pus from a pustule and smearing it into a cut made in the skin of a healthy person. This produced a mild and immunising response from the body's immune system. British and Continental disdain for the practices of Colonials meant that the practice was ignored in the old world until 1714, when Timoni wrote about a similar practice that he had observed in Istanbul (Constantinople). When Lady Mary Wortley Montagu (1689-1762) returned from there, she was able to popularise the practice in Britain, where Queen Caroline (1768-1821) set the example by having her children inoculated. Since Queen Mary (1662-94) had previously died of smallpox, the impetus for some solution was vital. Although doctors continued to disapprove of preventative inoculation, the practice continued to spread and, by the 1990s, smallpox became the first major disease completely eradicated by man.

❖       ❖       ❖

While leprosy seems to have been more a state of mind than a physical ailment and smallpox was a killer of children and the 'uncivilised' peoples of the New World, one other medical surprise came upon Europe in the late medieval and early modern period. That was syphilis. From the 1490s, syphilis – the Great Pox – spread across Europe, starting in Italy, Spain and France. It is impossible to estimate the number of people infected by syphilis for two major reasons. First, many relatives and individuals attempted to hide cases of syphilis. Since it was identified very early on as a malady associated with illicit and immoral sex, evidence of infection was humiliating. Syphilis, unlike plague, was a disease that struck individuals and served as a public comment upon their character and behaviour. In so doing, syphilis replaced leprosy as an individual mark of sinfulness and gross immorality. Secondly, since the disease goes through three distinct stages and can take thirty or more years to kill a person, many sufferers may have died of some other complaint before the syphilis was able to kill them.

Western society had been able, with some difficulty, to construct a form of leprosy from their knowledge of the disease in ancient writers and the Bible. Plague, although not readily identifiable with anything in the great corpus of Greco-Roman medical and philosophical literature, was capable of conflation with previous

*An engraving of a syphilitic from the late
fifteenth century, by Albrecht Dürer.*

'plagues' at a conceptual level. Syphilis, however, was a new disease. Schooled to believe that there was 'nothing new under the sun' and that the ancient world was the pinnacle of human development, writers and learned men found it nearly impossible to believe that they were being afflicted with a novelty. As Niccolò Leoniceno (1428-1524), professor of medicine at Ferrara, wrote: 'I absolutely cannot believe that this illness is born suddenly only now and has infected only our epoch and none of the preceding'.

This meant that scholars and leaders were forced to explain the appearance of a new disease and its method of propagation. In the late fifteenth century, soon after its appearance, a number of reasons were advanced to account for syphilis. It was said that its appearance coincided with a conjunction of Jupiter and Saturn in 1484 – before the discovery of the Americas. As with plague, the conjunction of heavenly bodies was capable of producing an inimical response on earth. Others said that it was simply another type of leprosy. This had the great advantage of allowing for its easy classification and, pre-sumably, treatment. Some said that it was the result of lewd sexual practices. From the very beginning there seems to have been those who realised that the disease was connected with sexual behaviour.

The modern reader should not assume this meant that syphilis was understood to be a venereal disease transmitted through sexual contact though. It was visually obvious from its symptoms that syphilis was a disease of the sexual organs. It took little imagination to connect its physical impact on the genitalia with indecency. The proof that the disease was fundamentally misunderstood can be seen in two aspects of this analysis of its cause. First, it was assumed that syphilis could not be passed during licit sex (that is, between married people). Secondly, even into the nineteenth century, syphilitics were being advised to use prostitutes rather than mas-turbation, since the latter was seen as sexually 'more' deviant and therefore likely to exacerbate the condition.

Some authors even attempted to explain that syphilis was in some way connected to pork. Since Jews (and lepers) were known for not consuming pork, it was thought that there was some direct connection. Here, most dramatically, the confusion of disease, religion, and moral purity is most obvious. Jews and lepers were morally blemished in the minds of their Christian contemporaries. A new disease had appeared that attacked the genitalia (and was most visible on men). Jews and lepers were especially associated with immoral sexual practices. The connection seemed obvious and irrefutable. Ironically, there may be some truth in connecting the disease with animals in that many now assert that syphilis may have been a disease of sheep that managed to cross from one species (sheep) to another (man) as the result of sexual contact. While lewd sexual practices and animals may be at the root of the disease in man, Jews and lepers (confined respectively to urban ghettos or leper houses) are less likely as vectors for the disease than bored shepherds.

Although there were many explanations for the appearance of syphilis there was almost universal agreement on the means of its initial propagation. In 1494, the armies of the French King, Charles VIII (1470-98), were said to have carried the disease throughout central and northern Italy and thence to France. Henceforth, most people referred to syphilis as the 'French Disease'. The French alone rejected this nomenclature and constantly referred to it as the 'Neapolitan' or 'Spanish' disease. During its first few decades, syphilis killed dramatically, gruesomely and quickly. Normally, as mentioned above, the disease takes years to be fatal. There are many who suggest that initially the disease was accompanied by other non-venereal forms of syphilis such as yaws, which made the combined, cumulative impact of the disease more virulent. Following the trade routes of European merchants, syphilis quickly spread around the world. By 1504, syphilis was noted in Canton, where it was called the 'plum-tree ulcer'. William Clowes, a doctor at St Bartholomew's Hospital in London estimated that 50 per cent of incoming students, in 1585, were syphilitic.

The most damning explanation for the disease, and one that exists to this day, is that syphilis was a disease originating in the New

World. The association of a disease of sexual immorality with the 'uncivilised' and 'barbarous' peoples of the New World was very attractive. In 1526, Gonzalo Fernandez de Oviedo (1478-1577) in his *Natural History of the Indies* told the Spanish King that: 'Your Majesty may rest assured that this disease came from the Indians'. Non-venereal forms of the disease were certainly known in the New World and were treated by traditional methods involving guaiac wood. The wood, when thus identified, became a very valuable commodity and was widely imported into Europe to treat syphilis and other ailments as a virtual panacea. More importantly than Oviedo's identification of a possible treatment was his belief that the New World was the source of the disease. There appears to be no clear evidence of the venereal form of the disease being unique to the Americas. It is possible that the disease was actually a new development (rather as HIV/Aids is) or that is was a mutation of the non-venereal versions of the disease when they came in contact with a community (Westerners) who had had no contact with them before. If the latter is the case, then one can say that the West brought smallpox (a mild disease in Europe) to the Americas and returned with syphilis (a mild disease in the Americas). However, the evidence of transatlantic communication of syphilis is not as clear as with smallpox. Indeed, it would have had to have been a very virulent disease to have returned to Spain with Columbus in March 1493 and been able to infect the French army rampaging across Italy in 1494.

Eventually, Europe was able to assimilate this new disease and fit it into the traditional pattern of morality and malady. As Erasmus (*c.*1466-1536) noted in 1526, 'twenty-five years ago, nothing was more fashionable in Brabant [than public baths], today there are none, the new plague [syphilis] has taught us to avoid them'. Women, especially prostitutes, were seen as carriers of the disease and immoral sexual contact the means of spreading it. The most common treatment developed was the use of mercury as recommended by barber-surgeons and chemical medical practitioners. Mercury was rubbed into the body as a salve or ingested directly.

This early form of homeopathic chemotherapy was extremely dangerous. The patients' gums rotted and their teeth fell out, as did their hair. If the treatment was to work at all (and it probably had little therapeutic effect) it had to do so before it actually managed to kill the patient.

Two final epidemic diseases that appeared to spread and act like plague appeared in the late fifteenth and early sixteenth centuries as well. Like smallpox, malaria and yellow fever appear not to have been known in the New World prior to the arrival of the Europeans. However, the diseases appear to have come from Africa and were introduced to the Americas with slaves. Although neither disease managed to gain a foothold in Europe (apparently for climatic reasons), Europeans were as likely to die in large numbers from both when they came in contact with them. Indeed, it appeared that only Africans were relatively immune to both as was noted and commented upon by contemporaries. The mild form of malaria (*vivax malaria*) found in Europe was not as virulent as that found in Africa and the Americas (*falciparum malaria*). Where these diseases existed, they struck with extreme violence and mortality rates were normally about 25 per cent. Until adequate forms of treatment were developed in the twentieth century, these diseases continued to be a grave threat to life and limb. Indeed, in those countries that lack the financial and pharmaceutical clout of developed nations, both, especially malaria, remain plague-like and regularly kill many hundred of thousands if not millions each year.

Each of the diseases discussed above functioned in various societies as plagues. They attacked large numbers of individuals and evidenced extremely high mortality rates. Not every disease was equally virulent in each society. Inevitably, these diseases became associated with morality. Each was explained and assimilated into a context of religious and philosophical presuppositions. In most cases, Western communities attempted to apply the methods of segregation and quarantine to containing these plagues. Taken as a whole, they highlight the fact that plague was but one catastrophic, violent disease among many. The horror of plague was its cyclical and indiscriminate nature.

❖     ❖     ❖

There is, however, one other context in which plague needs to be located and that is in its wider historical setting. In the opening chapter of this book, the First Great Pandemic was discussed. The Black Death has been discussed as the opening outbreak of the Second Great Pandemic. The Marseilles plague of 1720 has, constantly and universally, been seen as the last European plague – the end of the Second Pandemic. The outbreaks of plague in the late nineteenth century are considered to be the start of the Third Great Pandemic. However, this view highlights the very narrowly focused definition of Europe by most (English-speaking) historians. Plague continued in parts of Europe well after 1720, and there is some reason for thinking that there was actually no clear break between the Second and Third Great Pandemics. A brief discussion of these later outbreaks will form the final element for understanding the context of plague.

Ironically, in 1743, plague struck Messina in Sicily, the accepted gateway for the Black Death in the 1340s. However, it had been raging in Eastern Europe (Ukraine, Hungary, Moravia, Austria and Poland) since 1738, continuing until 1744. In 1755-57, European Turkey and Transylvania were struck. A much wider outbreak of plague occurred in various nations of Eastern Europe: Moldavia, Wallachia, Hungary, Poland, Ukraine, Galicia, Kiev and throughout Russia (over 56,000 died in Moscow alone). Constantinople was beset by pestilence in 1778. Within a few years (1785), Transylvania, Slavonia and Livonia were seeing cases of plague. The Dalmatian coast (of the former Yugoslavia) was the scene of an outbreak in 1783-84. The century ended with plagues in Syria and Egypt (1799-1800).

Central Europe, in the form of the Austrian monarchy, took steps to prevent the further incidence of plague in the West. In 1739, they introduced an effective *cordon sanitaire* along their borders with the Ottoman Empire (European Turkey). Over 4,000 troops were permanently stationed along the borders with Slavonia, Croatia, Transylvania and the Danube. Stationary guard posts were supplemented by mobile bands of soldiers to keep the border hermetically sealed. Anyone attempting to sneak across the border was to be shot. Travellers and merchants arriving from Ottoman lands were expected to stop at the sentry posts. There, they were subjected to a complete physical examination to find buboes or any other signs of plague in their armpits and groins. Assuming they passed this exam they were then confined for a further forty-eight days. All their goods were fumigated. Bulk goods that might carry the infection (for example, raw wool and cotton) were stored in warehouses. Poor peasants were forced to sleep with the bales of merchandise for the quarantine period. If they developed the plague, they were to be shot and the goods burned.

Although this extreme form of quarantine and segregation seems to have worked, it did not stop the appearance of the plague in the Balkan Peninsula. In 1813, plague occurred in Bucharest, Bosnia and Malta. Two years later, in 1815, the Dalmatian coast and Corfu were struck. More worryingly (and the cause of a general panic), a few plague cases appeared in Noja in eastern Italy. In 1816, the fear of plague was eclipsed by the appearance in India of cholera, which reached Britain in 1832 and managed to replace plague as a mass killer of urban populations. By 1828-29, Greece (Morea), Moldavia, Wallachia and the Crimea were the scenes of plague outbreaks. A decade later, in 1840, Dalmatia was beset yet again. The following year, plague returned to Constantinople. As late as 1877-79, plague appeared in Baku on the Caspian Sea and along the Volga River in Russia.

On the edge of the Europe, plague was also a continuing problem. One example of the clash between plague control and bureaucratic realities was Egypt. In the late 1820s, Mehemet 'Ali Pasha (*c.*1769-1849) took control of the state from its (foreign) Mamluk overlords. He set up a comprehensive rural healthcare programme – something not equalled in Britain until after the Second World War. During an outbreak in 1834, he implemented the full range of 'Italian' plague regulations. However, local people resisted them with violence and determination. These methods were considered irreligious, as they appeared to be trying to avoid the will of God. Further, their implementation relied heavily on Western (infidel) doctors. Worse, the use of autopsies and alterations to burial customs limiting the number of mourners were extremely offensive to local sensibilities. Although 'Ali Pasha failed to control this plague outbreak, in 1841 he used armed troops to impose a harsh regime of plague controls. People were systematically examined for plague by being forced to strip and wash before medical workers (including female practitioners to examine women). After being declared healthy, they were dressed in new, clean clothes. This developing system and the general modernisation of the country eventually collapsed when Egyptian attempts to prohibit free trade by protecting national, monopolistic industries was opposed by Western states, who eventually forced the state to accept a less ambitious set of goals under the careful monitoring of Europeans.

What is clear from the above is that plague, while not endemic in Western Europe, was certainly a regular feature of life in parts of the Mediterranean Basin as well as the Balkans and Eastern Europe. The effectiveness of the Austrian barricades across the Balkan Peninsula might be debated, but they were certainly the ultimate manifestation of late medieval views on quarantine and segregation. Effectively, Western and Central Europe had managed, collectively, to create a *cordon sanitaire* around the whole of the area. Provisions and regulations originally designed in the mid-1400s for cities had been reshaped and altered to apply to the greater part of Europe. In short, Western and Central Europe had become a single urban community, administering a complete system of examination, segregation and quarantine.

The Third Great Pandemic appeared in the Orient and only briefly touched Europe or other 'Western' states. In 1894, plague broke out in Canton (killing about 100,000) and Yunnan Province in China. For the next five years, Hong Kong was repeatedly struck by plague, though only 6,272 deaths were reported. Although few actually died, the mortality rate among those infected was very high at 90 per cent. In 1896, Taiwan saw plague cases and, in 1899, Japan was struck. However, when the plague managed to transfer itself to India, the number of deaths increased dramatically. In 1898-1906, over 480,000 died (53,000 per year) in Calcutta and the Bengal Presidency. A further 1.2 million died in the Bombay Presidency during 1896-1906 (over 109,000 per year). In the other parts of India, an additional 2.1 million died (nearly 200,000 per year). Plague continued to be a major cause of death on the subcontinent; 12.6 million people died there in 1898-1948 (over 250,000 deaths per year).

This pandemic continued to follow the global trade routes. In 1899, there were 114 deaths in Portugal (Oporto) and a bizarrely isolated three deaths in Vienna. Australia saw a number of cases spread over many cities in 1900: Sydney (103 deaths), Adelaide, Melbourne, Brisbane, Rockhampton, Townsville, Cairns, Ipswich, Freemantle, Perth and Coolgardie. In the same year, there were fifteen deaths from plague reported in Glasgow, with an additional 363 dead in South Africa (Capetown and Port Elizabeth) in 1901. There was even a scare in San Francisco, though plague seems not actually to have been present. It would appear that this last pandemic (which some scholars of the Islamic world see as the last dramatic phase of the Second Pandemic) was unable to become endemic anywhere except the Indian subcontinent. As already discussed, the outbreaks in Hong Kong made it possible for the bacillus to be isolated and identified. In subsequent years, medical research was able to produce a serum capable of treating the disease with high levels of success. Nevertheless, plague remains endemic to rodent populations in India, China and the Rocky Mountains of the United States. Isolated cases of bubonic plague are still reported each year in these areas, though fatalities are

*The quarantine house erected at Port Said for Egyptian soldiers suffering from plague in 1882.*

extremely rare. Thus, just as plague left Western Europe with a 'bang', the Third Pandemic – with its impact on the subcontinent – proved, yet again, that plague was still able to strike human populations with virulence and high mortality. Medical technology and pharmaceutical developments may well be able to cope with a few scattered cases of plague, but they have yet to prove that they are capable of preventing, containing or curing a major outbreak.

# Eight

# DEATH'S LEGACY
## The Lasting Impact of Plague on the West

*Practical experience shows that the remedies used by medical doctors are useless and sometimes poisonous.*

Cardinal Gastaldi

hen Cardinal Gastaldi pronounced on the efficacy of medicine, he was undoubtedly speaking for generations of Western Europeans. Countless millions had seen the helplessness of medicine and its practitioners in the face of the relentless, recurring bouts of plague. Smallpox, malaria, yellow fever, leprosy and a host of other major and minor diseases and ailments also seemed to be unbeatable. The slow progress of science and medicine in the control of disease makes the medical triumphs of the late nineteenth and twentieth centuries all the more remarkable. However, the legacy of plague (and the other 'plagues') is that many people continue to fear an outbreak of some unknown, virulent and incurable disease. People continue to view medicine and doctors with suspicion and a degree of mistrust. It is one of the great ironies of history that, in the early modern period, the medical community was basically homeopathic and at war with the 'charlatans' of chemical medicine, while the present age is witness to the distrust and frequent vilification of homeopathic and traditional medicines by a medical elite committed to 'chemical' methods of treatment.

Moreover, modern, developed, affluent nations and societies have become accustomed to thinking that disease and diseases are capable of control and eradication. The much-trumpeted destruction of smallpox is perhaps the best example. It is rarely noted that smallpox, while a dangerous and deadly disease, was relatively straightforward to destroy. The vector (or host) for smallpox was man. Once men were vaccinated, the disease was effectively destroyed. However, many other diseases, plague being one of them, are shared by, and live in, both humans and animals. People share sixty-five diseases with dogs and a further fifty illnesses in cattle can be passed to humans. Almost as many are present in sheep and goats. Pigs have over forty shared contagions with man. Horses, along with rats and mice, have over thirty each and about two dozen are held in common with poultry. In other words, there are literally hundreds of diseases residing in animals that can, at a given moment, break out of those vectors and infect man. Just as worryingly, they can incubate and mutate in their animal hosts and present mankind with new and perhaps more virulent versions of themselves.

The two best examples of this dangerous phenomenon are HIV/Aids and BSE/New Variant CJD. The actual source of HIV is still debated, as is the point at which it first appeared in humans. The best and most widely-accepted theory is that it is a form of a disease native to monkeys in parts of Africa that, at some very recent point in history, began to infect humans. While many people in the developed world continue to think of it as a disease specific to small groups within the wider community (gay men and drug users), it is in reality a much more widely-diffused illness in the general human population. In some countries of sub-Saharan Africa, estimates suggest that upwards of one quarter of the population is infected. There is every reason to expect that this disease will, in the next fifty years, have a demographic impact on these countries. That is, despite high birth rates, there will be real declines in total population. Moreover, although HIV/Aids seems to be controllable by the most recent developments in drug technology, the treatments are cost-prohibitive for most people around the world and, more importantly, they simply control the disease rather than curing it. This 'new' disease that arose in animals and spread to the human population has shown itself to be extremely adaptive and virulent. It remains fatal. Its one saving grace is that it cannot be transmitted very quickly or widely in a given population, since it requires the direct exchange of bodily fluids to pass from one person to the next.

New Variant CJD is, as its name suggests, also a novelty. There seems to be complete agreement that this disease developed in cattle with the appearance of BSE (Mad Cow Disease). This latter is, in itself, a new disease and would appear to be the direct result of alterations to methods of animal husbandry. Exactly how BSE is transmitted to humans in the form of New Variant CJD is still hotly debated. The best guess is that it comes through the ingestion of nerve tissue from cows. Like HIV/Aids, this new disease is always fatal. In addition, there is no current method of treatment nor, in its earliest stages, any way of diagnosing the disease. However, it appears that it cannot be passed from one person to the next.

The appearance of both of these diseases has already begun to have a profound impact on historical interpretations of plague and other past diseases. Traditionally, attempts to explain the sudden appearance and disappearance of certain diseases, as well as their tremendous destructive power through mutation, have been rejected or, at least, considered suspect. That is less the case now. Many more people are now willing to accept that syphilis, for example, is a relatively recent mutation from non-venereal diseases such as yaws. The sudden onslaught and departure of plague, many now admit, might well be the result of changes to the disease itself, rather than to any activities of man in altering his environment and hygiene. If anything, the appearance of two new highly-dangerous, degenerative diseases has caused historians to be much less optimistic about the role of man in the alterations of patterns of health and epidemic mortality in the past. Both HIV/Aids and New Variant CJD are reminders to modern man of the creative ability of nature to be destructive. These new plagues have led modern people to develop a new interest in the plagues – and the plague – of history.

❖     ❖     ❖

What are the lasting consequences of plague? Most would accept that the demographic collapse of the late fourteenth and early fifteenth centuries forced Western Europe to make substantial alterations to the socio-economic realities of the day. Fewer workers, many argue, required innovation and labour-saving devices. The ability of people to leave their farms for the supposedly better pay and conditions of the towns and cities meant the acceleration of the collapse of the feudal system (already teetering towards its demise). A decline in demand for grains meant that land could be put to other uses, such as grazing and the production of wool. Thus, the economy of Western Europe was shocked out of a routine and stability that might have led to it remaining a predominately agrarian society, wedded to subsistence farming.

On the social level, plague exacerbated the persection and scapegoating tendencies already present in Western European society. Outsiders and those who were different were viewed as possible sources of infection and disease. Cleanliness – especially of the soul and mind – both at the individual and communal level, was held to be an essential element of disease prevention. The toleration of diversity became almost synonymous with the toleration of sinfulness. Pollution meant anything that was different and healthiness meant purity and conformity. Most of these trends existed before the plague and have their roots in the ideology of Crusade and Holy War. Nevertheless, plague and other epidemic diseases gave power to the imagery and, more importantly, gave it a reality and importance in each and every community. Pollution could exist anywhere and had to be rooted out if plague was to be avoided.

Plague and the development of the regulations for its control have also left a profound imprint on the modern Western mind. Quarantine and segregation are, for most people, the immediate and natural response to any unknown disease. Indeed, they often remain the response even when the disease is known and understood. For example, fear of contamination by, and infection from, HIV/Aids has led to some calls for the quarantining (in those of a charitable mind) of everyone carrying the disease. Some more enthusiastic supporters of medieval methods have suggested that members of 'high risk' groups should be segregated. Moreover, despite the best advice of science and medicine, many people still believe that the disease can be passed through any of a number of means, from door handles to clothing. HIV positive children are driven from schools and non-infected individuals from the 'high risk' groups (rather like Jews in the fifteenth century) are targeted for violence and discrimination as polluted and infectious. HIV/Aids is regularly called the modern plague, and the response of people time and again mirrors the actions and reactions of their late medieval and early modern ancestors.

Another peculiarity of the response to modern epidemics is the unwillingness of many people to believe that the medical community and the state actually know what they are doing. BSE/New Variant CJD has revealed a whole range of behaviours very like those of plague days. For example, what Cardinal Gastaldi failed to add is that most people had also come to the conclusion that official state remedies (in the form of regulations) were equally ineffective. Not only that, but the bureaucratic response to plague was motivated largely by a desire to control and stabilise society and the economy. Individuals regularly disobeyed plague legislation for reasons of personal profit and economic survival. Time and again, the officials and leading members of society cheated at the margins or, as often as not, flagrantly and openly for the benefit of their own purses.

There can be little doubt that BSE came into being and was allowed to flourish because of changes to animal husbandry driven by economic motives. It has been shown that the state and individuals frequently downplayed the extent of the problem for economic reasons. British officials now find their beef boycotted and blockaded by most other nations and consumers. In effect, British beef is being subjected to regulations developed in the 1400s. Just as plague-infected states often tried to keep their trading partners from discovering that they had plague cases, the British state tried to downplay the extent of BSE. Despite the unanimous opinion of scientific and medical advisors that the situation has been resolved, other bureaucracies and individuals continue to demand the blockading of British beef. Many in Britain argue that this is less because of health fears and more to protect home markets from external competition. As the French might say, while refusing entry to a lorry-load of British beef: 'the more things change, the more they stay the same'.

An even more dramatic example of the enduring grip of plague and plague regulations on the modern mind occurred in the early 1990s. The world was shocked to learn that there was a suspected outbreak of bubonic plague in western India in the region of Mumbai (Bombay). The astonishing enthusiasm with which the developing world cut all travel and trade with the whole of India is instructive and illuminating. Mumbai is a long way from Calcutta, but flights from both were suspended. Pakistan is probably closer to Mumbai, but flights from there were still allowed. The reaction was the quarantining of a nation-state (India), with little or no regard to geography. Moreover, all scientific advice was that the supposed outbreak was confined to a small rural area and unlikely to involve anyone who might find themselves on a flight to the West. It was also pointed out that the length of flights from the subcontinent would probably allow for the incubation of the disease and the appearance of symptoms. Hence, no cases were likely to get past the normal immigration and customs checks already in existence. Nevertheless, the West attempted to interpose a *cordon sanitaire* between itself and India.

The very mention of 'bubonic plague' produced a panic at the popular and official level capable of negating every word of advice coming from scientists and doctors. Regularly in the Rocky Mountains there are cases of bubonic plague, and yet there are not regular bans on travel from Colorado, let along the whole of the United States. Indeed, part of the panicked response may well have been associated with attitudes to India as a country with a less developed medical infrastructure. That is, prejudice and attitudes of the 'other' seem to have lain carefully and quietly behind a façade of concerns about health. The pristine, healthy West had to be protected from possible infection arising in a polluted, insanitary developing country. The reaction was illogical and unnecessary, but wholly intelligible when seen in the historical context of reactions to plague and other epidemic diseases as they developed in the West.

Plague and other diseases of a pestilential nature have left a profound impact on the psyche of the West. Purity became the opposite of pollution. Healthiness and cleanliness were given an interpretation that transcended the natural and physical to include the moral and spiritual. Doctors were seen as, at best, well-meaning incompetents, and, at worst, as dangerous charlatans. Governmental officials were viewed as self-serving bureaucrats more interested in social stability and their own livelihoods than public welfare. Health regulations became matters of personal choice to be obeyed only when it suited an individual. Scientific and medical 'fact' was, and is, treated as opinion by politicians and the general public alike. The poor and the dirty have remained as carriers of disease and contagion.

Perhaps the greatest legacy of plague is the memory of its destructive power. Fear is the abiding inheritance of four centuries of pestilence. Fear of disease, fear of pollution, fear of outsiders, fear of diversity, fear of doctors, scientists and politicians. Sealed in their homes by the state, abandoned by clergy and physicians, cowering on their sickbeds, Westerners learned to distrust and fear the potent power of plague and most attempts to prevent it. If they learned anything, it was that the correct response to plague was harsh and draconian quarantine or speedy flight. People feared plague and pestilence, and they still do. Plague as a medical disease may no longer be a threat to the stability of society or the life of the individual, but as a social construct and a powerful memory it is still able to send an advanced, progressive community fleeing into its fortress, looking for infectious scapegoats to expel. Thanks to plague and epidemic disease, cleanliness is still next to godliness and moral diversity remains physically dangerous. Healthiness, purity and sanitary remain concepts as deeply entwined with the metaphysical, the moral, and the spiritual as they do with medicine, science and sanitation.

# BIBLIOGRAPHY AND
# ADDITIONAL READING

Acidini-Luchinat, C., *Renaissance Florence* (Milan, 1993).

Alexander, J., *Bubonic Plague in Early Modern Russia* (Baltimore, 1980).

Anselment, R., 'Pox', in *Seventeenth Century* 4: 2 (1989): 189-211.

Appleby, A., 'Epidemics and Famine in the Little Ice Age', in *Journal of Interdisciplinary History* 10: 4 (Spring, 1980): 643-63.

Appleby, A., 'The Disappearance of Plague: A Continuing Puzzle', in *The Economic History Review* 33 (2): 161-83.

Arrizebalaga, J., *The Great Pox: The French Disease in Renaissance Europe* (New Haven, 1997).

Baldwin, M., 'Toads and Plague: Amulet Therapy in Seventeenth-Century Medicine', in *Bulletin of the History of Medicine* 67: 2 (Summer, 1993): 227-47.

Barker, R., 'The Local Study of Plague', in *Local Historian* 14: 6 (May, 1981): 332-40.

Barolsky, P., 'Cellini, Vasari and the Marvels of Malady', in *Sixteenth Century Journal* 24: 1 (1993): 41-5.

Baron, H., *In Search of Florentine Civic Humanism* (Princeton, 1988).

Barroll, J., *Politics, Plague and Shakespeare's Theatre* (Ithaca, 1992).

Barry, J., *Witchcraft in Early Modern Europe* (Cambridge, 1996).

Behringer, W., *Witchcraft Persecution in Bavaria* (Cambridge, 1997).

Beik, W., 'Elite Repression', in *Journal of Interdisciplinary History* 11: 1 (1980): 97-103.

Beilin, E.V., Redeeming Eve: *Women Writers of the English Renaissance* (Princeton, 1987).

Bennett, J., *Women in the Medieval Countryside* (Oxford, 1987).

Bertrand, J., *Historical Relation of the Marseilles Plague, 1720* (Farmborough, Hants., 1973).

Biagioli, M., 'The Social Status of Italian Mathematicians, 1450-1600', in
  *History of Science* 27 (1989): 41-95,

Biller, P., *Heresy and Literacy, 1000-1530* (Cambridge, 1994).

Bostridge, I., *Witchcraft and its Transformation c. 1650-1750* (Oxford,
  1997).

Boswell, J., *Christianity, Social Tolerance and Homosexuality* (Chicago, 1980).

Bowsky, W., 'The Impact of the Black Death upon Sienese Government
  and Society', in *Speculum* 39:1 (Jan 1964): 1-34.

Bray, A., *Homosexuality in Renaissance England* (London, 1982).

Briggs, R., 'Women as Victims? Witches, Judges and the Community', in
  *French History* 5: 4 (Dec., 1991): 438-50.

Briggs, R., *Witches and Neighbours* (London, 1996).

Brockliss, L. W. B., *The Medical World of Early Modern France* (Oxford,
  1997).

Brucker, G., 'Bureaucracy and Social Welfare in the Renaissance: A
  Florentine Case Study', in *Journal of Modern History* 55: 1 (March,
  1983): 1-21.

Brundage, J., *Law, Sex and Christian Society in Medieval Europe* (Chicago,
  1990).

Brundage, J., *Sumptuary Laws and Prostitution in Late Medieval Italy*
  (Amsterdam, 1987).

Buhler, S., 'Marsilio Ficino's De Stella Magorum and Renaissance Views
  of the Magi', in *Renaissance Quarterly* 43 (1990): 348-71.

Bullough, V., *Handbook of Medieval Sexuality* (New York, 1996).

Bullough, V., *Sexual Practices and the Medieval Church* (Amherst, 1984).

Burnby, J., *A Study of the English Apothecary 1660-1760* (London, 1983).

Burnett, J., 'Medicine Chest', in *Medical History* 26: 3 (1982): 325-33.

Bynum, C., *Holy Feast and Holy Fast: The Religious Significance of Food to
  Medieval Women* (Berkeley, 1987).

Calvi, G, 'Florentine Plague', in *Representations* 13 (1986): 139-63.

Carmichael and Silverstein, 'Smallpox', in Journal of the History of
  Medicine and Allied Sciences 42: 2 (1987): 147-68.

Carmichael, A., 'Contagion Theory and Contagion Practice in Fifteenth-
  Century Milan', in *Renaissance Quarterly* 64:2 (Summer, 1991): 213-56.

Carmichael, A., *Plague and the Poor in Renaissance Florence* (Cambridge, 1986).

Carroll, L. L., 'Carnival Rites', in *Sixteenth Century Journal* 16: 4 (1985): 487-502.

Cattelona, G., 'Control and Collaboration', *French Historical Studies* 18: 1 (1993): 13-33.

Chrisman, M., 'From Polemic to Propaganda: The Development of Mass Persuasion in the Late Sixteenth Century', in *Archiv für Reformationsgeschichte* 73 (1982): 175-96.

Chrisman, M., *Lay Culture, Learned Culture* (New Haven, 1982).

Cipolla, Carlo M., *Cristofano and the Plague* (London, 1973).

Cipolla, Carlo M., *Faith, Reason and the Plague in Seventeenth Century Tuscany* (Brighton, 1979).

Cipolla, Carlo M., *Fighting the Plague in the Seventeenth Century* (Madison, Wisc., 1981).

Cipolla, Carlo M., *Public Health and the Medical Profession in the Renaissance* (Cambridge, 1976).

Clark, J., *The Dance of Death in the Middle Ages and Renaissance* (Glasgow, 1950).

Clark, S., 'The "Gendering" of Witchcraft in French Demonology: Misogyny or Polarity?', in *French History* 5: 4 (Dec., 1991): 426-37.

Clark, S., *Thinking with Demons: The Idea of Witchcraft in Early Modern Europe* (Oxford, 1997).

Cohen, J., *The Friars and the Jews: The Evolution of Medieval Anti-Judaism* (Ithaca, 1982).

Cohen, S., *The Evolution of Women's Asylums since 1500* (Oxford, 1992).

Cohn, S., *Women in the Streets: Essays on Sex and Power in Renaissance Italy* (Baltimore, 1996).

Collino, M., *The Dance of Death in Book Illustration* (Columbia, Missouri, 1978).

Collins, J, 'Economic Role of Women', in *French Historical Studies* 16: 2 (1989): 436-70.

Conrad, L., 'Epidemic Disease in Formal and Popular Thought in Early Islamic Society', in Ranger and Slack, eds, *Epidemics and Ideas* (Cambridge, 1992): 77-99.

Copenhaver, B., 'Scholastic Philosophy', in *Renaissance Quarterly* 37: 4 (1984): 523-54.

Crawford, J., 'Attitudes to Menstruation', in *Past and Present* 91 (1981): 47-73.

Cuvillier, J., 'Economic Change, Taxation and Social Mobility in German Towns in the Late Middle Ages', in *Journal of European Economic History* 15: 3 (Winter, 1986): 535-48.

Daly, K., 'Four Aspects of the Renaissance', in *European Historical Quarterly* 17: 1 (1987): 79-85.

Daniel. W., *The Black Death: The Impact of the Fourteenth Century Plague* (Binghampton, NY, 1982).

Davidson, N., 'Rome and Venetian Inquisition', in *Journal of Ecclesiastical History* 39 (1): 16-36.

Davies, J., *Florence and its University during the Early Renaissance* (Leiden, 1998).

Debus, A.G., 'Paracelsians', in *Ambix* 28: 1 (1981): 36-54.

Debus, A.G., *The French Paracelsians: The Chemical Challenge to Medical and Scientific Tradition in Early Modern France* (Cambridge, 1991).

Deutscher, T., 'Episcopal Tribunal of Novara', in *Catholic Historical Review* 77: 3 (1991): 403-21.

Dingwall, H., *Physicians, Surgeons, and Apothecaries: Medicine in Seventeenth-Century Edinburgh* (East Lonton, 1995).

Dixon, L., *Perilous Chastity: Women and Illness in Pre-Enlightenment Art and Medicine* (Ithaca, 1995).

Dols, M., 'The Second Plague Pandemic and its Recurrence in the Middle East: 1347-1894', in *Journal of the Economic and Social History of the Orient* 22:2 (1979): 162-89.

Dols, M., *Black Death in the Middle East* (Princeton, 1997).

Donegan, J. B., *Women and Men Midwives* (Westport, 1978).

Douglas, M., *Witchcraft Confessions and Accusations* (London, 1970).

Eamon, W., 'Science and Popular Culture in Sixteenth Century Italy: The "Professors of Secrets" and their Books', in *Sixteenth Century Journal* 16: 4 (1985): 471-85.

Edgerton, S., 'Icons of justice', in *Past and Present* 89 (Nov 1990): 23-38.

Edgerton, S., *Pictures and Punishment: Art and Criminal Prosecution during the Florentine Renaissance* (Ithaca, 1985).

Edwards and Spector, *The Olde Daunce: Love, Friendship, Sex and Marriage in the Medieval World* (Albany, 1991).

Edwards and Ziegler, *Matrons and Marginal Women in Medieval Society* (Woodbridge, 1995).

Edwards, J., *The Jews in Western Europe, 1400-1600* (Manchester, 1994).

Eliav-Feldon, M., 'Secret Societies', in *Journal of Medieval and Renaissance Studies* 14: 2 (1984): 139-58.

Ell, S., 'Iron in Two Seventeenth Century Plague Epidemics', in *Journal of Interdisciplinary History* 15:3 (Winter, 1985): 445-57.

Ell, S., 'The Interhuman Transmission of Medieval Plague', in *Bulletin of the History of Medicine* 54 (4): 497-510.

Elliott, D., *Spiritual Marriage: Sexual Abstinence in Medieval Wedlock* (Princeton, 1993).

Erler, S., 'Printing of Galen', in *Huntington Library Quarterly* 48: 2(1985): 159-71.

Fabricius, J., *Syphilis in Shakespeare's England* (London, 1994).

Ferrari, G., 'Public anatomy', in *Past and Present* 117 (1987): 50-106.

Ferreiro, A., *The Devil, Heresy and Witchcraft in the Middle Ages* (Leiden, 1998).

Fleischer, M., '"Are Women Human?" – The Debate of 1595 between Valens Acidalius and Simon Gediccus', in *Sixteenth Century Journal* 12: 2 (1981): 107-20.

Gavitt, P., *Charity and Children in Renaissance Florence: The Ospedale degli Innocenti, 1410-1536* (Ann Arbor, 1990).

Ginzburg, C., *Ecstasies: Deciphering the Witches' Sabbath* (London, 1990).

Ginzburg, C., *The Night Battles* (London, 1983).

Goldberg, P. J. P., 'Mortality and Economic Change in the Diocese of York, 1390-1514', in *Northern History* 29 (1988): 38-55.

Goldberg, P. J. P., *Women, Work and Life Cycle in a Medieval Economy* (Oxford, 1992).

Goodman, J., 'Financing Pre-Modern European Industry', in *Journal of European Economic History* 10: 2 (1981): 415-35.

Gottfried, Robert S., *Epidemic Disease in Fifteenth Century England* (Leicester, 1978).

Gottfried, Robert S., *The Black Death. Natural and Human Disaster in Medieval Europe* (Macmillan, 1983).

Gregory, A., 'Witchcraft', in *Past and Present* 133 (1991): 31-66.

Grell, O., 'Plague in Elizabethan and Stuart London: The Dutch response', in *Medical History*, 34 (1990): 424-39.

Haas, L., *The Renaissance Man and his Children: Childbirth and Early Childhood in Florence 1300-1600* (Basingstoke, 1998).

Hackenberg, M., 'Books in Sixteenth Germany', in *Journal of Library Studies* 21: 1 (1986): 72-91.

Hall, W., 'Country General Practitioners', in *Local History* 20: 4 (1990): 173-86.

Harlay, D., 'The Beginnings of the Tobacco Controversy: Puritanism, James I, and the Royal Physicians', in *Bulletin of Medical History* 67 (1993): 28-50.

Haselkorn, A., *Prostitution in Elizabethan and Jacobean Comedy* (Troy, NY, 1983).

Hatcher, J., *Plague, Population and the English* (London, 1977).

Henderson, J., 'Society and Religion', in *Historical Journal* 29: 1 (1986): 213-25.

Henderson, J., 'The Parish and the Poor in Florence at the Time of the Black Death: The Case of S. Frediano', in *Continuity and Change* 3:2 (1988): 247-72.

Henderson, J., *Piety and Charity in Late Medieval Florence* (Oxford, 1994).

Henningsen, G., *The Witches' Advocate* (Reno, 1980).

Herlihy, David, *The Black Death and the Transformation of the West* (Harvard, 1997).

Hester, M., 'Dynamics of Male-Domination', in *Women's Studies International Forum* 13: 1-2 (1990): 9-19.

Hester, M., *Lewd Women and Wicked Witches* (London, 1992).

Hickey, D., 'Local Hospitals', in *Social History* 25: 49 (1992): 9-33.

Hoffman, P., 'Land Rents and Agricultural Productivity: The Paris Basin, 1450-1789', in *Journal of Economic History* 51:4 (Dec. 1991): 771-805.

Hopkins, D., *Princes and Peasants: Small Pox in History* (Chicago, 1983).

Horden, P., 'Disease, Dragons and Saints: The Management of Epidemics in the Dark Ages', in Ranger and Slack, eds, *Epidemics and Ideas* (Cambridge, 1992): 45-76.

Horrox, R., ed., *The Black Death* (Manchester, 1994).

Hsia and Lehmann, *In and out of the Ghetto: Jewish-Gentile Relations in Late Medieval and Early Modern Germany* (Cambridge, 1995).

Hughes, D., 'Distinguishing Signs: Earrings, Jews and Franciscan Rhetoric in the Italian Renaissance city', in *Past and Present* 112 (Aug. 1986): 3-59.

Hults, L., 'Baldung and the Witches of Freiburg: The Evidence of Images', in *Journal of Interdisciplinary History*, 18: 2 (Autumn, 1987): 249-76.

Hults, L., 'Baldung's Bewitched Groom Revisited: Artistic Temperament, Fantasy and the 'Cream of Reason', in *Sixteenth Century Journal* 15: 3 (1984): 259-79.

Hunter and Hutton, *Women, Science and Medicine 1500-1700* (Stroud, 1997).

Huppert, G., *After the Black Death* (Bloomington, 1986).

Jackson, R., *Doctors and Diseases in the Roman Empire* (London, 1988).

Jonathan and Goldberg, *Queering the Renaissance* (London, 1994).

Jütte, R., 'Ageing and Body Image in the Sixteenth Century: Hermann Weinberg's (1518-97) Perception of the Ageing Body', in *European History Quarterly* 18: 3 (July, 1988): 259-90.

Jütte, R., 'Seventeenth Century German Barber-surgeons', in *Medical History* 33: 2 (1989): 184-98.

Karant-Nunn, S., 'Continuity and Change: Some Effects of the Reformation on the Women of Zwickau', in *Sixteenth Century Journal* 13: 2 (1982): 17-41.

Karlen, A., *Plague's Progress: A Social History of Man and Disease* (London, 1996).

Karras, R., *Common Women: Prostitution and Sexuality in Medieval England* (Oxford, 1996).

Keefer, M., 'Agrippa's Dilemma: Hermetic "Rebirth" and the Ambivalence of De vanitate and De occulta philosophia', in *Renaissance Quarterly* 41 (1988): 614-53.

Kent, J., 'Population Mobility', in *Local Population Studies* 27 (1981): 35-51.

Klapisch-Zuber, C., *Women, Family and Ritual in Renaissance Italy* (Chicago, 1985).

Krekic, B., 'Abominandum Crimen', in *Viator* 18 (1987): 337-45.

Kritzman, L., *The Rhetoric of Sexuality and the Literature of the French Renaissance* (Cambridge, 1991).

Kuehn, T., *Law, Family and Women: Toward a Legal Anthropology of Renaissance Italy* (Chicago, 1991).

Labalme, P., 'Sodomy and Venetian Justice', *Tijdschrift voor Rechtsgeschiedenis* 52: 3 (1984): 217-54.

Langholf, V., *Medical Theories in Hippocrates* (Berlin, 1990).

Lansing, C,. *Power and Purity: Cathar Heresy in Medieval Italy* (Oxford, 1998).

Lindley and Ormrod, eds, *The Black Death in England, 1348-1500* (Stamford, 1996).

Local Population Studies, *The Plague Reconsidered: A New Look at its Origins and Effects in Sixteenth and Seventeenth Century England* (Matlock, 1977).

Mack, A., *In Time of Plague: The History and Social Consequences of Lethal Epidemic Disease* (New York, 1991).

Martensen, R., '"Habit of Reason": Anatomy and Anglicanism in Restoration England', in *Bulletin of the History of Medicine* 66: 4 (Winter, 1992): 511-35.

Martin, J., 'A Warwickshire Town in Adversity: Stratford-upon-Avon in the Sixteenth and Seventeenth Centuries', in *Midland History* 7 (1982): 26-41.

Masten, J., *Textual Intercourse: Collaboration, Authorship, and Sexualities in Renaissance Drama* (Cambridge, 1997).

Mathers, C., 'Family Partnerships and International Trade in Early Modern Europe: Merchants from Burgos in England and France, 1470-1570', in *Business History Review* 62: 3 (1988): 367-97.

McNeill, W., *Plagues and Peoples* (Oxford, 1977).

McVaugh, M., *Medicine before the Plague* (Cambridge, 1993).

Menning, C., 'Loans and Favours', in *Journal of Modern History* 61: 3 (1989): 487-511.

Mentzer, R., 'Organizational Endeavour and Charitable Impulse in Sixteenth-Century France: The Case of Protestant Nîmes', in *French History* 5: 1 (Mar., 1991): 1-29.

Moran, B., 'Christoph Rothmann, the Copernican Theory and Institutional and Technical Influences on the Criticism of Aristotelian Cosmology', *Sixteenth Century Journal* 13: 3 (1982): 85-108.

Moran, B., 'Conceptions of Time', in *Sixteenth Century Jounal* 12: 4 (1981): 3-19.

Moran, B., 'German Prince-Practitioner', in *Technology and Culture* 22: 2 (1981): 253-74.

Moran, B., 'Hermetic-Alchemical Circle', in *Ambix* 32: 2 (1985): 110-26.

Moran, J., 'Clerical Recruitment in the Diocese of York, 1340-1530: Data and Commentary', in *Journal of Ecclesiastical History* 34: 1 (Jan., 1983): 19-54.

Murray, J., 'Agnolo Firenzuola on Female Sexuality and Women's Equality', in *Sixteenth Century Journal* 22: 2 (1991): 199-213.

Naphy and Roberts, *Fear in Early Modern Society* (Manchester, 1997).

Netanyahu, B., *Toward the Inquisition: Essays on Jewish and Converso History in Late Medieval Spain* (Ithaca, 1997).

Nicholas, D., *The Domestic Life of a Medieval City: Women, Children and the Family in Fourteenth Century Ghent* (Lincoln, Neb., 1985).

Nicholson, W., *Historical Sources of Defoe's Journal of the Plague Year* (London, 1969).

Nikiforuk, A., *The Fourth Horseman: A Short History of Epidemics, Plagues and other Scourges* (London, 1993).

Oakley, A., *The Captured Womb: A History of the Medical Care of Pregnant Women* (Oxford, 1984).

Otis, L. L., *Prostitution in Medieval Society* (Chicago, 1985).

Pagel and Winder, From Paracelsus to Van Helmont (London, 1986).

Pagel, W., Paracelsus: An Introduction to Philosophical Medicine in the Era of the Renaissance (Basel, 1982).

Pagel, W., *The Smiling Spleen: Paracelsianism in Storm and Stress* (Basel, 1984).

Park and Daston, 'Unnatural Conceptions: The Study of Monsters in Sixteenth- and Seventeenth-Century France and England', in *Past and Present* 92 (1981): 20-54.

Park, K., *Doctors and Medicine in Early Renaissance Florence* (Princeton, 1985).

Pearl, J., 'French Catholic Demonologists and their Enemies in the Late Sixteenth and Early Seventeenth centuries', in *Church History* 52 (1983): 457-67.

Pelling, M., 'Occupational Diversity: Barber-Surgeons and the Trades of Norwich, 1550-1640', in *Bulletin of the History of Medicine* 56: 4 (1982): 484-511.

Perkins, W., 'Midwives v Doctors: The Case of Louise Bourgeois', in *Seventeenth Century* 3: 2 (1988): 135-57.

Perkins, W., *Midwifery and Medicine in Early Modern France: Louise Bourgeois* (Exeter, 1996).

Phillips, E., *Aspects of Greek Medicine* (Philadelphia, 1987).

Polizzotto, L., *The Elect Nation: The Savonarolan Movement in Florence 1494-1545* (Oxford, 1994).

Potter, D., 'Marriage and Cruelty among the Protestant Nobility in Sixteenth-Century France: Diane de Barbançon and Jean de Rohan', in *European History Quarterly* 20: 1 (Jan., 1990): 1-38.

Pugh, W., 'Testamentary Charity', in *French Historical Studies* 11: 4 (1980): 479-504.

Pullan, B., 'Support and Redeem: Charity and Poor Relief in Italian Cities from the Fourteenth to the Seventeenth Century', in *Continuity and Change* 3:2 (1988): 177-208.

Quetel, C., *History of Syphilis* (Cambridge, 1990).

Ramsey, M., 'Environment', in *Journal of Interdisciplinary History* 19: 4 (1989): 611-19.

Ranger and Slack, *Epidemics and Ideas: Essays on the Historical Perception of Pestilence* (Cambridge, 1992).

Rashkow, I., *Upon the Dark Places: Anti-Semitism and Sexism in English Renaissance Biblical Translations* (Sheffield, 1990).

Rawcliffe, C., 'Medicine and Medical Practice', in *Guildhall Studies in London History* 5: 1 (1980): 13-25.

Roberts, A., 'The Plague in England', in *History Today* 30 (Apr): 29-34.

Roberts, N., *Whores in History* (London, 1993).

Rocke, M., *Forbidden Friendships: Homosexuality and Male Culture in Renaissance Florence* (Oxford, 1996).

Roe, D. A., *A Plague of Corn: The Social History of Pellagra* (Ithaca, 1973).

Rogal, S., 'Medical Journals', in *British Studies Monitor* 9: 3 (1980): 3-25.

Romano, D., 'Domestic Service in Renaissance Venice', in *Sixteenth Century Journal* 22: 4 (1991): 661-77.

Roper, L., 'Common Man, Common Good, Common Woman', in *Social History* 32 (1986): 19-43.

Roper, L., 'Prostitution', in *History Workshop Journal* 19 (1985): 3-28.

Roper, L., *Oedipus and the Devil: Witchcraft, Sexuality and Religion in Early Modern Europe* (London, 1994).

Rose, M., *The Expense of Spirit: Love and Sexuality in English Renaissance Drama* (Ithaca, 1991).

Rossiaud, J., *Medieval Prostitution* (Oxford, 1988).

Rothkrug, L., 'Holy Shrines, Religious Dissonance and Satan in the Origins of the German Reformation', in *Historical Reflections* 14: 2 (1987): 143-286 .

Rowland, J., *Swords in Myrtle Dress'd: Towards a Rhetoric of Sodom* (Madison, 1998).

Rubin, M., *Gentile Tales. The Narrative Assault on Late Medieval Jews* (New Haven, 1999),

Ruggiero, G., *The Boundaries of Eros: Sex Crimes and Sexuality in Renaissance Venice* (Oxford, 1985).

Rushton, P., 'Lunatics and Idiots', in *Medical History* 32: 1 (1988): 34-50.

Rushton, P., 'Women, Witchcraft and Slander', in *Northern History* 18 (1982): 116-32.

Russell, P., 'Syphilis, God's Scourge or Nature's Vengeance', in *Archiv für Reformationsgeschichte* 80 (1989): 286-306.

Saslow, J. M., *Ganymede in the Renaissance: Homosexuality in Art and Society* (New Haven, 1986).

Sella, D., 'Coping with Famine: The Changing Demography of an Italian Village in the 1590s', in *Sixteenth Century Journal* 22: 2 (1991): 185-97.

Shatzmiller, J., *Jews, Medicine and Medieval Society* (Berkeley, 1994).

Shrewsbury, J., *History of Bubonic Plague in the British Isles* (Cambridge, 1970).

Shrewsbury, J., *The Plague of the Philistines* (London, 1964).

Siegel, R., *Galen's system of Physiology and Medicine* (Basel, 1968).

Siraisi, N., 'Girolamo Cardano and the Art of Medical Narrative', in *Journal of the History of Ideas* 52: 4 (1991): 581-602.

Siraisi, N., *Medieval and Early Renaissance Medicine* (Chicago, 1990).

Slack, P., *The Impact of the Plague in Tudor and Stuart England* (Oxford, 1990).

Steel, D., 'Plague Writing: from Bocaccio to Camus', in *Journal of European Studies* 11 (1981): 88-110.

Stewart, A., *Close Readers: Humanism and Sodomy in Early Modern Europe* (Princeton, 1997).

Stromer, W. von, 'Commercial Policy and Economic Conjuncture in Nuremberg at the Close of the Middle Ages: A Model of Economic Policy', in *Journal of European Economic History* 10: 1 (Spring, 1981): 119-29.

Taylor, J., 'Plague in the Towns of Hampshire: The Epidemic of 1665-6', in *Southern History* 6 (1984): 104-22.

Terpstra, N., 'Piety and Punishment: The Lay Conforteria and Civic Justice in Sixteenth-Century Bologna', in *Sixteenth Century Journal* 22: 4 (1990): 679-94.

Trachtenberg, J., *The Devil and the Jews* (Philadelphia, 1983).

Traister, B., '"Matrix and the Pain thereof": A Sixteenth Century Gynaecological Essay', in *Medical History* 35 (1991): 436-51.

Uitz, E., *The Legend of Good Women: Medieval Women in Towns and Cities* (Mt Kisco, 1990).

Ungerer, G., 'George Baker: Translator of Aparicio de Zubia's Pamphlet on the "Oleum Magistrale"', in *Medical History* 30 (1986): 203-11.

Walker and Dickerman, '"A Woman under the Influence": A Case of Alleged Possession in Sixteenth-Century France', in *Sixteenth Century Journal* 22: 3 (Fall, 1991): 535-54.

Walker and Dobson, *Barbers and Barber-Surgeons of London* (Oxford, 1970).

Walter, J., *Famine, Disease and Social Order in Early Modern Society* (Cambridge, 1989).

Warner, M., *Alone of all her Sex: The Myth and Cult of the Virgin Mary* (London, 1990).

Watts, Sheldon, *Epidemics and History: Disease, Power and Imperialism* (New Haven, 1997).

Webster, C., *From Paracelsus to Newton: Magic and the Making of Modern Science* (Cambridge, 1982).

Webster, C., *Paracelsus confronts the Saints: Miracles, Healing and the Secularization of Magic* (Oxford, 1995).

Webster, C., *Paracelsus on Natural and Popular Magic* (Rome, 1993).

Week, A., *Paracelsus: Speculative Theory and the Crisis of the Early Reformation* (Albany, 1997).

Weir, A., Images of Lust: Sexual Carvings in Medieval Churches (London, 1986).

Wensky, M., 'Women's Guilds in Cologne in the Later Middle Ages', in *Journal of European Economic History* 11: 3 (Winter, 1982): 631-50.

Westman, R., 'The Astronomer's Role in the Sixteenth Century: A Preliminary Study', in *History of Science* 28 (1980): 105-47.

Williman, Daniel, *The Black Death. The Impact of the Fourteenth Century Plague* (Binghampton, NY, 1982).

Wind, B., *A Foul and Pestilent Congregation: Images of 'Freaks' in Baroque Art* (Aldershot, 1998).

Wood, M., 'Paltry Peddlers or Essential Merchants? Women in the Distributive Trades in Early Modern Nuremberg', in *Sixteenth Century Journal* 12: 2 (1981): 3-13.

Wright, W., 'A Closer Look at House Poor Relief through the Common Chest and Indigence in Sixteenth Century Hesse', in *Archiv für Reformationsgeschichte* 70 (1979): 225-37.

Zguta, R., 'The One-Day Votive Church: A Religious Response to the Black Death in Early Russia', in *Slavic Review* 40:3 (Fall, 1981): 423-32.

Ziegler, P., *The Black Death* (New York, 1969).

Zika, C., 'Hosts, Processions and Pilgrimages: Controlling the Sacred in Fifteenth-Century Germany', in *Past and Present* 118 (Feb., 1988): 25-64.

# LIST OF ILLUSTRATIONS

# PICTURE SECTIONS

1 A seventeenth-century interpretation of the plague which befell the Philistines at Ashdod. (Wellcome Library)

2 War, pestilence and famine. (Wellcome Library)

3 Renaissance view of the plague in Phrygia. (Wellcome Library)

4 Account of the outbreak of plague in 1348 from the *Nuremberg Chronicle*. account of the outbreak of plague in 1348. (Stonyhurst College, photograph: P. Ansell)

5 Annotations on a page of ancient Irish laws, attributed to St Patrick.

6 An English version of a treatise on plague written by Jean de Bourgogne, which he dates as 1365.

7 Illustration from the annals of Gilles de Muisit, showing the burial of plague victims at Tournai in 1349. (Wellcome Library)

8 A Mass for the Dead, from a printed Book of Hours. (Stonyhurst College, photograph: P. Ansell)

9 Inscription from Ashwell church in Hertfordshire.

10 A watercolour of a wooden carving representing the clergy and people of Lyons calling upon God for deliverance from the plague in the fifteenth century. (Wellcome Library)

11 A priest administers the last rites to a dying man. (Stonyhurst College, photograph: P. Ansell)

12 Lithograph based on a mid-fifteenth-century painting by Bonfigli, showing the Virgin Mary responding to the intercession of saints and protecting people from the arrows of disease. (Wellcome Library)

13 Engraving by Dürer of a flagellant, 1510.

14 For the skeletons who have shadowed the living through life, their time has come as the living (depicted as horsemen) are forced to give up a life of pleasure. (Stonyhurst College, photograph: P. Ansell)

15 A talisman to ward off plague from a fifteenth-century leech book. (Wellcome Library)

16 The burning of Jews from the *Nuremberg Chronicle*. (Stonyhurst College, photograph: P. Ansell)

17 England's first Sanitary Act.

18 A pictorial broadsheet depicting the measures used to deal with the 1656 plague in Rome. (Wellcome Library)

19 A bird's-eye view of the pest house at Leiden in the Netherlands. (Wellcome Library)

20 St Carlo Borromeo, bishop of Milan, ministering to the city's plague victims during 1576. (Wellcome Library)

21 The frontispiece of Thomson's *Loimotomia* on how to dissect a pestilential victim.

at Genoa. (Reproduced with permission of Special Collections, Aberdeen University Library)

33  A skeleton representing death brandishes an arrow at a young couple. The man raises his arm to protect the woman beside him. (Reproduced with permission of Special Collections, Aberdeen University Library)

34  In a page from the Placebo, part of the Mass for the Dead. (Reproduced with permission of Special Collections, Aberdeen University Library)

35  An illuminated page from an early fifteenth-century Mass for the Dead shows the service taking place. (Reproduced with permission of Special Collections, Aberdeen University Library)

36  A Dutch manuscript version of the Mass for the Dead. (Reproduced with permission of Special Collections, Aberdeen University Library)

37  The martyrdom of St Sebastian from a manuscript Book of Hours which belonged to the bastard daughter of the French King Louis XI. (Stonyhurst College, photograph: P. Ansell)

38  The martyrdom of St Sebastian, from an early sixteenth-century manuscript connected with la Sainte Chapelle in Paris. (Stonyhurst College, photograph: P. Ansell)

39  The plague saints: St Sebastian and St Roch. (Stonyhurst College, photograph: P. Ansell)

40  Burning Jews, in an illustration from the *Nuremberg Chronicle*. (Stonyhurst College, photograph: P. Ansell)

# INDEX

# DARK HISTORIES

A series of books exploring the darker
recesses of human history.

## SERIES EDITOR

William Naphy, Senior Lecturer and
Head of History at the University of Aberdeen

## PUBLISHED

P.G. Maxwell-Stuart, *Witchcraft: A History*
'combines scholarly rigour with literary flair'
*The Independent on Sunday*

William Naphy & Andrew Spicer, *Plague*
'A chilling warning from history'
*The Sunday Telegraph*

William Naphy, *Sex Crimes*
'A model mix of of pin-sharp
scholarship and deep empathy'
*The Guardian*

## COMMISSIONED

P. G. Maxwell-Stuart, *Wizards: A History*

Further titles are in preparation.